# ANZI
# BEACHH
## DIARY OF A SI

CW01560608

## by *TOM ROE*

Foreword by SIR HARRY SECOMBE, CBE., D.Mus.

1

*ISBN* 0 951321404

© 1988
**REPRINTED 1993**
T. ROE

*Typeset & printed by;* Castle Graphics
Chesterfield, Derbyshire.

3

This book is dedicated to the Comradeship of the 8th Army, and in particular to my old buddies, Charlie, Bob and John.

*"Memory will mature in the garden of the mind, and, if one is a good gardener, memory will bloom. "*

*Edward Seago*    *War Artist*

*From " With the Allied Armies in Italy ".*

# FOREWORD

Many books have been written about World War Two by the leading participants - Alexander, Montgomery, *et al*, but the conflict as seen by the supporting players, the Gildensterns and Rosencranzes is far less well documented. My old mate, Spike Milligan, has written much about his walk-on part in battles, but he is an exception. There is still a large gap to be filled, in the literature describing how the average 'squaddy' saw things. Bewildered by events, most of the time unaware of the way the battle was going, bombarded with rumours, he carried on doing what he was told even though he might grumble about doing so. I know, because I was one of them!

Gunner Roe was one too, and his memoirs shed a welcome light on how it was for those of us who served in the ranks in North Africa and Italy. He writes extremely well, with humour and poignancy about his experiences. When I first read his manuscript I was completely caught up in the action, partly because his Army career closely paralleled mine - Territorial soldier, gunner, service in the same battle areas - but also because it is a very lucid narrative.

This is really a fine book and I recommend it as a true and graphic account of the day to day life of a soldier on and off the battlefield.

*Yours most sincerely,*
Sir Harry Secombe, CBE.. D.Mus.

# PREFACE

This story is not a catalogue of my heroic deeds in World War 2 and therefore comes nowhere near an epic story of valour, like "The Wooden Horse".

Nevertheless I can recall a few incidents which occurred to me on the long trek from Egypt to the top end of Italy, when my subconscious ego murmured "you should get a medal for that, or at least a mention. " In common with many others on the ground floor level of Army ranking there was never, just never, a person of Higher Authority around to witness my outstanding contribution towards winning the war. That's how it went.

My story has a two-fold purpose and I unfold them in sequence.

Ever since the end of the war the thought has been hammering at me that the story of Anzio beachhead should be told by a ranker who had been there, on a beleaguered beachhead for four months, from January to May, 1944. A story far removed from the recitations from the War Diaries of the Higher Echelons (much as they seem to be preferred by publishers) of cold statistical detail as they describe their juxtapositioning of one battalion with another battalion and one division with another division on the military chessboard.

Historians should write about Anzio again and again; so that a proper tribute can be paid to the indomitable courage of the infantrymen lying up, in atrocious weather conditions, in the wadis in front of the Flyover Bridge, between Carroceto and Campoleone. Every infantryman at Anzio deserved a medal as big as a frying pan - as the saying goes - and every single battalion deserved a special citation.

My second purpose, and just as important, was the need to portray the thoughts, the hopes and the fears which ran through the mind of the ordinary squaddy while on active - and I mean active - service.

In this I hope that I have succeeded.

T.R.

# LIST OF ILLUSTRATIONS

# CONTENTS

*A 25 pounder gun position*

# CHAPTER ONE
## "Sunday best - battledress, gaiters and hobnailed boots"

On 10th July, 1941 the progress of the war took a distinct turn for the better.

The arrival of the postman, slotting a long envelope headed O.H.M.S. through the letter box, changed an ordinary day into a Special day. Turning the envelope over in my hands I conjectured about the contents although, as I thought about it afterwards it would have been better to have opened it right away.

I shouldn't have been surprised as information had been bandied about that, the war situation being what it was, the age band for reserved occupations in certain categories of job was being revised.

Being a mere pen-pusher for a railway Company I was one of the favourites to be scooped up into the net

The contents were short in text but explicit in detail. It was an invitation on behalf of His Majesty's Government to present myself for my first military rendezvous at the Boythorpe Road Drill Hall in Chesterfield for a medical examination.

As I passed through the portals of the Drill Hall on the a I ppointed day I had very mixed feelings. "Things must be in a pretty pickle in this war to want an old man like me." I thought at thirty two you can feel pretty ancient at times.

At the behest of the examining doctor I dropped my trousers and coughed. Up to then I had always thought you only coughed when you were poorly; this military order to cough showed me the other side of the coin; a good cough and you were three parts of the way to an Al grading.

Fastening up my buttons - zips were not plentiful - and guessing that the quality of my cough had got me three quarters of the way to an Al grading, - in spite of my varicose veins - I processed to the inner sanctum of the Recruiting Officer.

I was ushered into the small side office where the Military Presence sat in a chair. In my nervous state I thought I was

11

confronted by a Colonel. I found out later that he was only a Second Lieutenant; an equivalent grade to the sanitary orderly orthe Cookhouse Joe if you compared officer ranks with squaddy ranks.

Nevertheless credit where it was due. By a good encircling movement right at the start he outflanked me. As I thought about it - as I did four eventful years later - the possibility was there that he won the war by the simple question which followed at 10. 30 a. m. on July, 10th 1941.

"I see that you are a clerk on the railway. What does that mean exactly?" he asked.

"Oh, it means a lot of things. I issue passenger tickets. I collect tickets, I make balance sheets - two each month. One for passenger traffic, the other for Goods traffic. I stick parcel stamps on waybills for chums of milk sent by local farmers on the 7.15 a.m. train each day. I make out grain-sack hiring tickets when the farmers send their grain to market. I prepare waybills for every wagon of coal which leaves the pits we cater for with wagons. I am a daily sufferer from writer's cramp. If I worked in a private organisation my clerical qualities would be recognised and I would be classified as an accountant. With the ability of the London and North Eastern Railway Co. to denigrate anybody who does not work in their corridors of power at Manchester, I am classified as a Booking Clerk while actually doing sixty per cent of Goods Traffic work, which includes the coal way-billing. "

"You like your work?" He put in.

"So, so. It's slavery at three pounds sixteen shillings and nine pence per week. You know what 1927 was like." When I said it I knew he didn't - he was too young to be facing it. "I waited eighteen months - well not waited. I worked down a pit. Then waited another ten years to find out if they were going to retain me. It was a long apprenticeship of uncertainty for a married man with a family. "

I felt that I could get up a head of steam in the conversation; a feeling encouraged by the fact that I was not yet wearing gaiters and forage cap.

"Very interesting," said the Recruiting Officer. "In a few minutes I've learned a lot about the London and North Eastern

Railway Co., "It's a good job you were a fast talker or my programme would have been in disarray."

"Thank you, sir" said 1, forgetting that I was not yet in the Forces.

There was a pregnant pause for a few seconds. Six seconds seems like a lifetime when you are waiting for the other fellow,"Oh, by the way. Apart from all that you have told me, do you know the Morse Code" he inquired disarmingly.

My ego, totting up a notch or two was my undoing. The warning signals in my brain were neither loud nor clear. The headlines about the Western Desert hadn't been too good of late and I wondered, passingly, if they wanted somebody to rectify the dismal situation.

"Yes, I do know the Morse Code," I said coming out of my reverie. "I understand Single Needle telegraphy."

That single sentence fixed me for the duration. He must have known that the Royal Artillery was short of signallers.

"Morse Code? dot dash; dash, dot, dot etc.," he interpolated?

"Yes, sir," said 1, forgetful once again of his military status and my civilian status.

"Do you have any preference? Army, Navy or Air Force?"

Not having given it much thought before 14th August, 1941, 1 hesitated momentarily, then settled the issue in my own mind.

"Yes, Navy" I fancied walking with a rolling motion from port to starboard and vice versa.

I left the building with more mixed feelings than when I arrived.

So naturally I got calling up papers for the Army, as a trainee signaller in the Royal Artillery and instead of wearing bell-bottom trousers, I started bashing out "Charlie, Charlie, Charlie" signals by lamp in a first initiation into the mysteries of Royal Artillery Fire Orders. We never did use a Helio lamp in passing messages.

Not too many days elapsed before I changed my travel warrant for a railway ticket at Chesterfield station. I was on my way to the 39th Signal Training Regiment at Nostell Priory. En route to life's most agonising experience; a change-over from family life to three weeks square-bashing as a rookie artilleryman. Tell me anything that comes harder than that.

I did three weeks square-bashing at Nostell Priory, confined to barracks all the time. Motor transport training - vehicles and motor bikes - at Heath Hall for five weeks, and the final course for Signallers at Bretton Hall.

The raw impact of the imposition of military power over civilian indulgence appeared in seconds on the first drill session, as Number 40 squad - composed of genteel ex-teachers, ex-bank clerks and ex-railway clerks, stamped the asphalt of the little courtyard until it hurt the ankles.

We knew we had surrendered our previously well-ordered lives to the autocracy of Authority albeit that Authority had on occasion, only the meagre allocation of two stripes, half-way between the elbow and the shoulder.

The future pattern of our lives was clearly illustrated when we were issued with palliasse covers, directed to a pile of straw and told to make our beds; so that we could lie on it.

An idle thought did a slow jig in my mind. "We'll be working like horses, so we're bedding down like horses. Wouldn't be surprised if we don't think that straw is our staple diet, after they'rethrough with us here."

In my first hours in an Army uniform I wised it out, in conference with myself, that unkind thoughts against officialdom were best kept as unofficial secrets, with only one person in the know; Number 1128308 Gunner (new) Roe, T.

I kept it that way for the rest of my unnatural life in the army.

So the screw turned tighter and tighter, day by day. At night my restless soul - except when on Guard Duty or Fire Picket (getting acquainted with the "two on, four off" procedure) counted the sheep on the "one, two three - one, one, two three - one" sequence from the Drill Manual; now being etched on my sub-concious mind. The numbers game was beginning to bite.

For three weeks Nostell Priory was pure, unadulterated misery.

The squad moved on to Heath Hall, on the outskirts of Wakefield, for the M.T. course - theory and practice - on vehicles and motor bikes. As my only previous personal experience of transport on wheels had been my three-speed push bike I envisage difficulties.

I was very unhappy that they occurred in the way they did.

The very first time I handled my potential weapon for an early demise, a 500 c.c. B.S.A. motor-bike, I fell over with it. We were not synchronised with each other and sheer weight was too much for a puny, ageing ex-penpusher like me.

Came the day when I did throw my right leg over the petrol tank with some confidence, adjusted my crash helmet and, with five others, emerged from the M. T. yard to the starting point of the "Kirkthorpe" circuit; which was Kirkthorpe church. Adjacent to the parade ground, it was the starting point. The "line of march" was, two experienced ones at the front, the instructor (I think it was Bombardier Bob Thornton; a nice guy) in the middle and the novices - including me -making up the rear; and so we set off.

Approaching Heath Common the instructor signalled for a U-turn and, with that signal, proved that I had been day-dreaming when the classroom lecture had been on 'Clutches, motor cycles, soldiers, for the use of."

At that decisive moment my thoughts must have been on the many things which were flooding thick and fast, through my unprepared mind just then; such as Guard Duties, Gas Drill, Fire Picket, kit inspection (lay out your "smalls" to table knife length - PT kit to full battle - dress in three minutes, fatigues. etc.

Oh, the list was endless.

In a moment of mental aberration, fool that I was, instead of easing out the clutch slowly I released it straight out. I shot forward, out of control and in a panic; and found myself running in the ditch alongside the hedgerow.

I hadn't the slightest knowledge of what to do, but the first telegraph pole had a ready answer. Wham! I smashed into it.Hooray for crash helmets; I escaped with severe concussion. Could have been a lot worse.

Lugged into the back of a truck I went back to billets. And then saw enough daily medicals to evade the rest of the motor-bike course. Never in the Army again, would I throw my right leg over the petrol tank of a motor-bike and therefore classification as a Despatch Rider was out.

Don't think that made me miserable.

Such was the imbecility in high places at Heath Hall that a

bastard vehicle - a Fordson with the accelerator in the middle - was planted in a clutch (no pun intended) of six training vehicles ranging from 15 cwts. to 3 tonners lined up on the roadside.

On my passing-out day I wondered how many lamp posts had been pushed over and whether the death rate among the population of Wakefield had increased through the dithering of rookies feet, from the 39th Signal Training Regiment, searching for the right pedal. And finding the accelerator instead of the foot brake.

This being mid-September the M.T. yard was ringed with huge trees populated by masses of ripe leaves, ready to fall. What really got my goat was sweeping up those leaves as they fell off the branches at twice the rate I could sweep them up.

The idea of this fatigue, blossomed in the mind of the corpulent BSM, with a figure like Oliver Hardy and who could throw a comic salute like Stan Laurel.

Goodness me, didn't we need some light relief just then. The Battery Sergeant Major supplied it when his right arm progressed on its wavy way from the horizontal elbow position to the official meeting joint; one inch above the right eye-brow.

I chortled inwardly about it from time to time all the way from Alamein to Lake Garda and beyond; to Civvy Street.

The message got through to me, loud and clear, that this futile exercise was listed as Army Discipline; and watch out for many more daft things to be catalogued under the same heading, in the future.

For the third, and final, phase of our training - the Signaller's course - we marched down the road to Bretton Hall, midway between Barnsley and Wakefield. The next three months were restful, compared to what had gone before. We were billeted in a country house surrounded by acres of rolling grassland and woods.

Maybe, after the eight weeks "conditioning" we had just survived we could - and did - appreciate Bretton Hall for its serenity.

The passing-out ceremony came on January 20th 1942, when we paraded on the gravel in front of Lord 'St. Oswald's house steps at Nostell Priory; after which we were available for transfer to a regular unit.

If it appeared that my ramrod style on parade made me look like a member of the Guard's Brigade, I hasten to correct a wrong impression. My webbing belts had been notched up two holes too many by a zealous Bombardier of the regular staff and I had no feeling in my arms.

On 29th January, 1942 1 was routed for onward passage to an operational unit. Just like a parcel.

In my case the posting was to 456 Battery, 78th Field Regiment (City of Edinburgh). I dreaded the time when a Sassenach, surrounded by Scottish fitba' fanatics, would have to endure the radio transmission of a Scotland versus England match.

About midnight that night, after a long tedious train journey, via Edinburgh, through an amalgam of the dirtiest weather, I arrived feeling lonely, at Dunblane, Perthshire, on the threshold of the Scottish Highlands.

To my pleasant surprise I found that the Orderly Bombardier who met me on the platform was nearly my next door neighbour. Anyway, as near as natives of South Yorkshire and Derbyshire adjoining could be as neighbours. He came from Stocksbridge on the southern Pennine moors.

Len Barraclough's helpfulness, to a man uprooted from family life, re-christened to a seven digit nonentity on a Nominal Roll and surviving (just) the first five months through the military mincing machine, was unforgettable.

I entered a very strange world indeed when I was posted to a regiment with a different accent, different dress (thinking about the kilt), different food (thinking about the haggis) and to different musical sounds (thinking of the bagpipes). Just then I couldn't make common cause with any of their national attributes.

I soon found out that Hogmanay was 1st January and ritual, and that although salted porridge was also a Scottish ritual which made ordinary men into caber tossers it always happened that the natives of Glasgi and Auld Reekie were first past the post for sugared porridge. It didn't pay a Sassenach to linger abed.

Och aye, I had arrived.

The Bombardier took me in hand and it didn't take me long during the five minutes walk from the railway station to the Battery Office to realise he was a good guy.

17

Leaving the Battery Office, where I had been logged fo inclusion in future Nominal Rolls and Ration Indents, his Yorkshire humour surfaced as we walked across the Parade Ground which I learned afterwards was the playing pitch of Dunblane Football Club. "You're going to a Stately Home, ground floor. It belonged to an Earle ... the cement people. You'll be dossing on the concrete floor of this Nissen Hut tonight. Sorry, but it will only be for one night, until we get you properly billeted. Cheerio. "

"Cheerio, Bom, thanks," I replied. Funny thing you said "Yes, Bom," to the guy with stripes if you respected him and you said "Yes, BombardIer," if he was an unpleasant sod.

I never slept a wink that night. The Perthshire draughts, closing in from the Grampians, slid under the ill-fitting doors and through the ill-fitting windows. They easily had the edge on the heated stove pipe which although doing its best was not good enough. And what good were two blankets on such a night, seeing that half of one had to be on the cement floor.

It started a long acquaintanceship of sleeping on Mother Earth in an Army greatcoat.

As I said, "Och aye. " The foreigner had arrived!

On 4th July, 1942 the clipped precise voice of Major Cohn Arthur Pattullo, Battery Commander, carrying over the parade ground at Fyvie, twenty five miles north, north east of Aberdeen and sitting in the rural peace of the River Ythan ushered in another era for me. For what he was about to utter I shall always be profoundly grateful. It introduced me to my future buddies, and I never regretted his selection.

The old hands - and this being a Territorial regiment there were quite a few - and the new arrivals (of which I was one) soon realised the deep significance of the Battery Commander's briefing as one more important step to a war footing for the Regiment, particularly as we had just been kitted out with Shorts, (K.D.) and tried on pith helmets; which we never wore! We thought it hardly likely we would be going to Iceland, one of our northern outposts, in a pith helmet; ... although we never quite knew. Anything to do with Quartermasters always had a 'but'. However, as sandy locations around Egypt were hogging a good share of the newspaper headlines mental guessing games were the fashion.

"The Establishment of Freddy Troop, 456 Battery 78th Field Regiment, Royal Artillery will be as follows:- "Robert "Freddy, O.P. truck. Captain J. Alton, Troop Commander; Gunner Maycock, A. O.P. Ack; Gunner Henretty W., Driver; Gunner Signaller Hutton, R. Wireless Operator.

George Freddy, Captain Baker, W. T. G.P.O.; Bombardier Queree, G.P.O. Ack; Gunner Signaller Harder, C. R. Wireless Operator; Roe, T. Gunner Signaller, Wireless Operator.

Monkey Truck . . .

The B.C.'s voice trailed away with the continuing Battery postings and I relegated him, with a wary eye on Jock Cardownie, the Battery Sergeant Major, to the background. I had realised some time ago that an uncontrolled twitch of the eyes could receive, at the least, an extra fatigue duty. Like a careless twitch at an auction sale which could land one with an unwanted item, I was very careful.

I mused how Baker, W. T., (Captain) Queree, (Bombardier) and Harder C. R., (fellow wireless operator) would really mix with me. Queree, at the same time was no doubt poring over Baker, Harder and Roe. I could guess that Baker, W. T. Captain and Gun Position Officer would be wrinkling his forehead and pondering how the shower of unknowns posted to George Freddy, d thrown into his lap, would sort out.

So the ex-prison Warden, - the eternally optomistic P.T. fiend -took charge of the Bank Clerk, the Railway (dock) clerk and the Railway (trains) clerk. He should have been clapped in his own peacetime gaol for a stretch, for his foolish expectations, later on, that his musclebound ageing minions would be able to unbend to the extent of doing a cartwheel, which was his speciality.

So on 13th July, 1942 my real travelling days began from Fyvie and proceeded apace, via the troopship the Empress of Japan. From the word 'go', like Jerome K Jerome's gang, except that we had four in the boat, the George Freddy team dipped their oars in unison over the Libyan desert and soldiered on in harmony. So harmoniously that, a year on, the balding Bombardier's hair started to grow a feathery fluff and the Captain's unruly but attractive thatch never lost a strand; we caused them so little trouble. Together we roamed the highways and byways from Port Tewfik to the Garigliano, and well beyond.

# CHAPTER TWO
### The Invasion of Italy. Introduction to Spaghetti and Polenta.

Leaving behind - awash in our memories - El Alamein, Mersa Matruh, Tmimi, Mareth, Gabes, Kairouan, Takrouna, Enfidaville, Sfax, Sousse, Syracuse, Milazzo and parting company from the 1st Armoured Div., 10th Armoured Div., 10 Corps, 4th Armoured Div., 4th Indian Div., 5th Agra., 6th Agra., some of whom no doubt would be calling for our help again, we crossed the Straits of Messina on 15th September, 1943.

Our invasion charge into Italy was marked with a near-miss with a landmine about a couple of miles from Reggio. The tank tracks of Robert Freddy, second in line of the Troop convoy (we were third) took the brunt of the impact. Luckily with minimal damage.

It was a clear moonlight night as we passed through Scylla, a deserted window-shuttered ghost village at 2 o'clock on the morning of 15th September. My tired eyes acknowledged defeat so, ignoring 'Dicky Dickinson's inexperience at the wheel, I fell asleep stretched out on the hood top of the Humber; prepared to buy the consequences.

Scylla, Bagnara, - the village where the Amazon women were reputed to carry the kitchen table on their heads when moving home - Palmi, and Rosarno were left behind. We moved slowly, in sight of the sea, through the rough Calabrian country. Nicotera, Tropea on the wild coast road led us to Sambiese and to a photographer's shop at Nicastro. A rare, rare event. Just beyond Pizzo higher authority decided that enough was enough so we leaguered at Nicastro.

For once in a while Charlie Harder, Bob Hutton, John Hayter and myself, who had soldiered on more or less together since Nostell Priory days - although John was in Edward Troop - were free from duty and decided to have a look at the village of Nicastro. Not that there appeared to be anything unusual there.

Italian villages always seemed to be perched on hill tops but this one sat in a valley, on a winding minor road approximately

21

twelve miles from Catanzaro, the ancient capital of Calabria. An unusual thing about our little group of signallers; we were all temporarily ex-Railway. Two from the Southern Railway (docks) and two from the London and North Eastern Railway.

To mark the occasion, spotting a photographer's shop, w decided to recce the position and if he was in business we'd part with a few lire. The event was momentous.

After verbal exchanges, pidgin Italian on our side, the photographer said "Si, si" and placed us in the typical family group system; two sitting and one standing at the back, exactly in the middle. Disappearing under the blanket covering the camera tripod he clicked the shutter. I can't remember if he said "say formaggio" (cheese) or not.

Arranging to go back in two hours, we explored the village. Eventually, we went back and collected the prints. Charlie's elongated face, etched in small folds by the retrospective sweaty grime of Wadi Akarit and other troublesome spots, was topped with a thin thatch of coarse matted hair which, on combing, would have tested the strength of a horse rake. His size eleven boots were coated with a goodly layer of vineyard dust; as indeed ours were. A pair of scraggy knees seemed to be the focal point holding the apparition together. The yellow dust on his uniform could have indicated return from a foray with the Chinese army. His K.D. shirt hung loosely in untidy folds, with one very creased edge being untidily draped over his left thigh and the other drifted over his right knee cap. The absence of three buttons destroyed all resemblance that his upper garment should have borne to a K.D. shirt.

The heat of the Western Desert and Sicily had spirited away a goodly portion of our body-meat, leaving only our bones. While the clarity of the group photograph paid tribute to the skill of the village photographer our skinny frames indicated that urgent action from the cookhouse wallahs was an essential ingredient for our rehabilitation.

Charlie said, a few weeks later that his mother wept when she received a copy of the photograph. It was no surprise to me, I could have cried myself. Charlie had not been so yellow since absorbing the choking dust of the desert as we moved into position for the barrage at El Alamein on 23rd October, 1942. We looked at each other then, novice soldiers in battle for the first time, and our expressions said "whither goest we". It was not long before we knew.

My haggard jockey weight, topped with a pinched little face and bearing no glorification to the constant M and V rations, was inadequately camouflaged by the cold steel rims of my Army issue spectacles. I added no distinction whatever to the photographic group of three 8th Army soldiers; temporarily at leaguer rest.

John Hayter was the dandy of the trio. He wore his forage cap with distinction, tip at the correct angle, and just the regulation distance above the right eyebrow. He was the only one to sport a belt. Apart from his K.D. shirt which looked as if it had been folded in small squares and then slept on by an elephant, our buddy from Edward Troop was O.K.

I thought afterwards "that photographer had his buttons on; putting the Beau Brummel of the trio at the back, standing at the viewers eye-level. "

At Nicastro I received a parcel from home. A bulky one, just the sort to attract attention from a small group of by-standers; gunner and signallers.

"Parcel for Roe" yelled the post orderly, in a voice loud enough to alert the whole Brigade. A parcel from home was always an event but a bulky parcel was a big occasion.

"O.K., just the job," I replied, "my wife said she was sending me a cake. Smells of English baking. Hope its not been right round the Cape, like we did, or it might walk out and say "Buon Giorno. "

"Funny bugger, " muttered one twit "can't you get on with it. "

By this time the congregation, showing distinct interest, began to get a bit restless and sarcastic remarks, tinged with impatience. began to punctuate the commentaries.

"Bluddy slow you are, cutting a piece of string and unwrapping a piece of brown paper," said Taffy, from the Welsh valley. "Speed it up a bit, boyo. "

The expectant gleams in the eyes of the onlookers waned, in stages, as the contents saw the light of day.

Cherry Blossom boot polish followed the Colgates tooth paste the Brasso followed the writing paper and, yes, even the louse powder.

"Well that's the first time I knew that Cherry Blossom boot polish smells like English baking," muttered one Geordie lout,who was not really in my inner circle. "We live and learn."

"Say, 'Roe, write and tell your missus that this is the Artillery; not the Guards Brigade, all spit and polish. Although we do have to do our share" said Larry Larcombe, a signaller, who at birth had some knowledge of the sound of Bow Bells.

"Sorry about this, fellers. You see how it is, no cake. "Wai until I see her," I thought, stupidly, forgetting that imminent and future incidents could well cancel out this non-event in my mind before I held her in my arms again.

For the next ten days or so we moved north-east as a component part of 6th Agra. As testimony to the speed of the German retreat and our follow-up at Andria, ten miles inland from the Adriatic and at the tip of the Bari-Barletta-Andria triangle we found a haberdashery shop which had a good supply, among other things of silk stockings. Evidently Jerry had been in too hurried a retreat to loot it.

I huddled into a corner, took out my paybook and carefully assessed my financial position, as at September 26th 1943.

It worked out like this: -

| | |
|---|---|
| Balance in hand | £2 17s 6d |
| To add 92 days at Is 10d | £8 8s 6d |
| TOTAL | £11 6s Od |
| | |
| Army Savings Association | |
| 92 days at 6d | £2 6s Od |
| Comforts | £1 10s Od |
| Certificates | £6 10s Od |
| Certificates Interest | 16s Od |
| Cash | £1 14s 3d |
| | |
| GRAND TOTAL | £24 2s 3d |

The grand total looked grander when changing into lire, at four hundred to the pound.

So I-methodical me - listed in my little book, for posterity the contents of the two parcels of haberdashery I sent to my wife from Andria, in penance for my thoughts on the Nicastro cake episode.

In a matter of hours the stock disappeared - mainly legitimately by payment - As members of the 78th realised this was an oasis, where the price of a pair of silk stockings at 60 lire - the equivalent of three shillings - was a bargain.

On 31st October, we dug in at Spinete sitting astride the Biferno, the river barrier after Volturno and the Garigliano. At a height of 5,000 feet in the Central Appenines the days were cold and dreary under leaden skies, and the nights were agonising in their misery as the temperatures plummeted.

In the severe winter conditions there was a distinct slowing down of the Regimental moves from gun position to gun position; from olive grove to vineyard and vice versa. In the same month of October, 1943 we had, prior to Spinete, four different firing zones; at San Severo supporting 6th Agra (Army Group, Royal Artillery) San Martino supporting the 78th (Battleaxe) Division, Larino supporting the 5th (Yorks) Div. and Campobasso supporting the 1st Canadian Div.

Right away I had decided not to knock my head against the ramparts of Edinburgh Castle as the 78th, being a Territorial mob, had all the gaffers - Warrant Officers, Sergeants and Bombardiers, with Christian names like Jock, Andy, Alex and the like - had the insignias of Authority on the sleeves of their uniforms; crowns and stripes acquired through long sessions at Annual Camps and short sessions of weekend soldiering on Sherrifmuir and other training grounds adjacent to Edinburgh.

My peaceful intention paid off. I can only remember one entry on my Army Form 252. In the Western Desert at Tmimi, between Alamein and Tobruk. I poured petrol on the allegedly cold sand in the petrol tin cut-out which served as the fireplace for cooking and brew-ups. Far from being cold the sand was alive. Whoosh. The blazing tin stuck in my hand fro some time before I could sling it clear; right between the legs of a fellow signaller.

But that's another story.

At Spinete indoor accommodation in the shape of cattle barns and casas were at a premium, not that this was surprising seeing

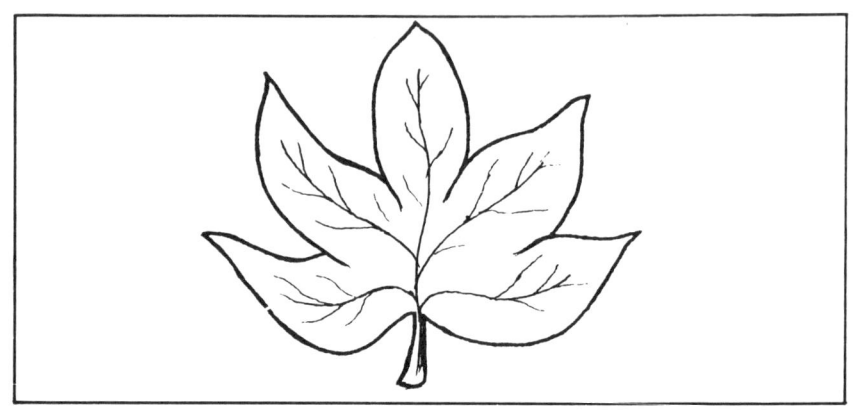

# 1ˢᵀ CANADIAN DIVISION
## OCTOBER 1943

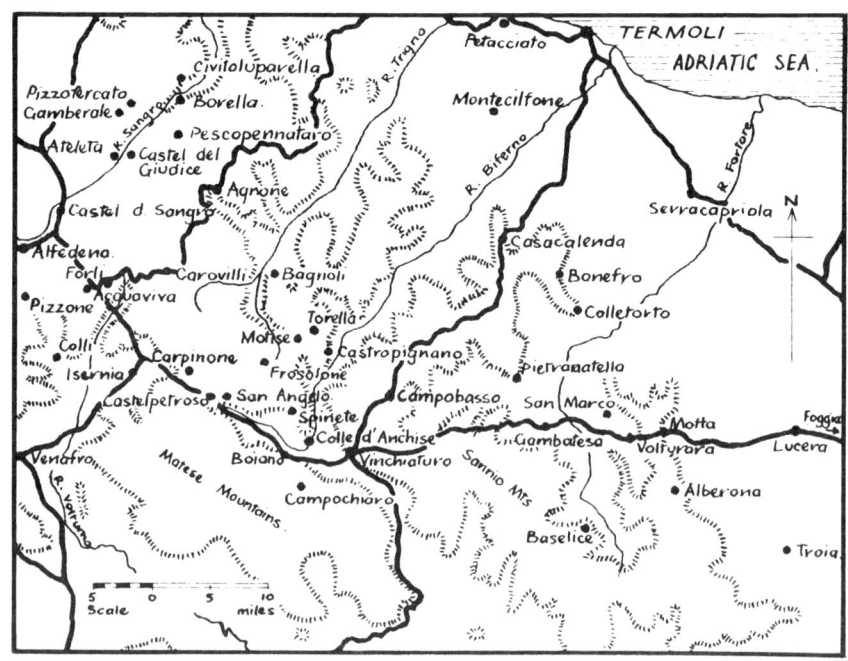

*The cold Abruzzi on the 1st Canadian Sector.*

that a sparsely populated peasant area, 5,000 feet up in the mountains, could hardly be expected to house in comfort all the Allied Divisions spread across the Appenines, east to west.

This time we were supporting the 5th (Yorkshire) Division. This happened to be the tenth higher formation we had fired our guns in anger for since the 1st Armoured Division started the habit at El Alamein on 23rd October, 1942.

There was little inclination to stand at the street corners and the chat talk was in the same bracket as the weather pattern; bleak, miserable and depressing. There was very little to be cheerful about on the 5th Div. front.

If any occupant of this miserable hole - no, not hole, mountainside - deserved a rum ration we did.

And one dram was the sum total of rum issue we did get; up front, anyway. And that a month overdue.

My stomach juices began to ferment and nasty thoughts paraded to the forefront as I pondered the situation. Strange it was that 1, a teetotaller, should get het-up about the absence of booze; but this was Spinete, five thousand feet up on the razor-back edge of the central Apennines. I would willingly have made a temporary recantation of my membership of the Temperance Society just to get some feeling into my bones.

And there was the principle of the thing.

Bearing in mind that military logistics indicated that - in a war situation - it took seven rear-echelon wallahs, at least, to support one up front. I wondered what my servants in the rear had done with my rum ration.

I visionised the procedure in the Quartermaster General's Supply and Demand department at Whitehall (or wherever).

First there would be a questionnaire (to be completed in quintuplicate) and this would start off something like this:

1) Is the temperature 30 degrees or thereabouts?
2) Have you had a rum ration before? If 'yes' say 'when' and 'where'. (The when is important as two rum rations, in close proximity, will place a great strain on the shipping resources.)

Footnote: Referring to paragraph I above 'thereabouts' only applies if it means 'less than' the figure quoted.

27

"When the form is completed and returned, the position will be carefully assessed."

My thoughts rata-tatted faster than the rate of fire from a machine-gun and they arrived at the Recruiting Officer at Chesterfield Drill Hall.

"I bet," I thought "that if, on the 10th July 1941 he had put me in my first choice - the Navy - by now I would have had rum galore. Every time the waves were twelve feet high and there was a swing over from port to starboard and back to port, more than normal their rule book would have allocated a ration of rum."

Mind you their line of communication was a lot shorter than ours; merely from the gallery to the decks; up a few stairs. Not like ours from Div. H.Q. to Regimental H.Q. to Battery H.Q. to Troop; over many miles. Up a few mountains and over a few rivers.

The Navy had another big advantage. When the rum arrived on the ship they were all in the same boat; they had no rear-echelon drains.

Spinete was one of the most miserable gun positions we had encountered so far. The steady rain and leaden skies poured dampness into my bones and it took its toll on 2nd November.

"Charlie, I can't get rid of the shivers. I feel lousy," I quavered.

"O.K. I'll keep an eye on you and have a word with Doughy. Naturally, with a surname like Baker, "Doughy" fitted. We had enormous respect for our boss.

When poorly, inward thoughts seem to jangle, cross each other's paths, get entangled and argue against each other. Mr. Freud had a reason for it, no doubt.

Mine started jangling. Some had a bit of sense, others worked at cross purposes; with stupid question and silly answer.

Like, "I've never been in hospital before in my life and I'm not so sure that I want to start now, especially in a military one. " - "Don't worry. Now's the time to start. " - . . . You're an idiot if you think that digging slit trenches and Command Posts, "mucking-in" in hovels, running out reels of Don 5 cable is better than a few days in "dock" . . . man, you are poorly. You've got a good case."

The next morning "Doughy" sent for the Medical Officer.

"Gunner Roe, is it? How do you feel?"

"Can't stop shivering, Sir. Been shaking like a jelly all night. "

"Stick this thermometer under your tongue. Hmm. your temperature is high. We'll send you back. Pack your small kit, be ready in half an hour."

Proceeding slowly the ambulance, of necessity - not because of me but because of the terrain - wended its way along the winding road from the hills and towards the eastern coastal sector. Somehow I felt a bit of a phoney; I always thought stretchers were for fellows with arms or legs off or for bad injuries.

I landed up at San Severo. It had been liberated recently, when we had supported 6th Agra.

"His temperature's very high," was the only thing I heard just then, as I lay on the stretcher on the floor of what could have been the local Town Hall. After six days my temperature had dropped to the vicinity of a normal 98 degrees and then four days convalescence followed.

After this, before I could say Sergeant Major, I was on my way back to renew acquaintance with Jock Cardownie in the sure knowledge that there would be a fatigue detail in his fist as soon as he saw me.

Before no time at all I was bedding down, again, on a cold marble floor. This one also hired from the Town Council, at Campobasso, and temporarily designated Transit Camp; on my way back to my unit in the line (we always seemed to be in the line). Still to be traced, no doubt about it, even after such a short absence the 78th Field would be digging in and tearing up some other poor padrones orchard for gun pits.

"Your unit the 78th Field Regt?" queried the orderly clerk at the Transit Camp, the agency for temporarily lost soldiers.

"Yes," I said, "it is", keeping the conversation to a tidy minimum.

"Never heard of that lot," said he, exhibiting in a few words bad taste and a lack of military geography. "Any ideas where they might be now?" he asked.

Not having been incorporated into the Intelligence Corps I could not put him out of his misery.

"Spinete, maybe, not far from here. That's where I left ten days ago."

"You really want to go back to your old mob then?"

29

"Yes, I want to get back to the 78th Field."

He turned round and went into the back office. Whether to have a conference with higher authority or to polish up his own Italian military geography I knew not.

The respite enabled me to have a quiet inward two-way conversation. I put the queries and I made the answers.

"Wouldn't like to separate from the lads now, would you? Even if you do think, on occasions, that the Troop Commander is a bastard, the R.S.M. a fugitive from the road sweeping section of Edinburgh City Corporation and that the Sergeant is over-burdened with big feet and no brains. Better the devil you know that the ones you have to be introduced to, in this life. "

In the midst of my Freudian thoughts the Orderly Clerk returned.

"Found out where 456 Battery is," I enquired.

"Yes, they're near Rionero approximately 45 miles north east from here. Transport has been laid on. Report here at eight o'clock in the morning with your kit. O.K.?"

So the following morning, in the back of a three tonner, I chugged back into the mountains. I might have been reporting back to Manchester on one of its worst days; except that Manchester had no high mountains like this province of Molise, of the alleged Sunny Italy.

Lowering rain clouds hovering over the mountain tops and playing hide and seek with each other compressed the atmosphere and restricted the chat of the four guys sitting in the back an looking at the murky countryside in reverse order. All going back to their own regiments and all going to different locations. All going back to the devils they knew and all going to the unknown.

At Rionero, in a river valley on a rainy day blistered by squalls of wind, where the mud was ankle deep, the guns bogged down boozy slime and the position harassed by sporadic German gunfire, I caught up with them again.

To my eternal shame the Troop Commander, the B. S. M. and the Sergeant welcomed me back.

I assuaged my conscience by persuading myself that only at displeasing incidents - to myself - had I described them so unkindly. They weren't a bad lot after all.

As if to celebrate my return, the following day the Naafi issue arrived.

Chocolate, 1 bar; Razor blades, 3; Soap, toilet, 1 bar; Writing paper; chewing gum; beer, 1 bottle; hardly constituted luxury but a

Naffi issue was always an oasis in a desert of shortages. It was so meagre that once again nasty thoughts about the surreptitious activities of the "Q" blokes cropped up again.

Then just as if the Germans were aware of the special occasion,-they opened up with fierce stonk into the valley. Trying to clutch three issues I went to ground. The slope of the ground, rising from the valley to the hilltop village, was rocky and hard with no top soil as a softener. I jarred every bone in my body.

When the enemy firing ceased, shaken in every nerve, I got back to the hilltop village. To hear tragic news.

Sergeant Len Barraclough and Larry Larcombe, the cheery Cockney signaller had been caught in the shellfire and killed. We were shattered.

It was the same Len Barraclough who had met me at Dunblane .railway station at midnight on 29th January, 1942, to set me on my way with a Scottish Regiment, with a thistle and No. 337 as their vehicle identification mark. His help on my posting night when, with my morale at zero and at a time when I needed a shoal of it, was tremendous. It eased the pangs of separation from "my ain folk".

He will always have a corner in my memories.

For some days the experts in rumour-mongering, the latrine marshals, had been passing on snippets of inspired information regarding regimental orders of march. Army tradition always put the latrine wallahs at the top of the league as harbingers of news. The grapevine source was pretty fruitful in quantity. Unfortunately the so-called good bits usually turned out duff while the adverse ones invariably turned out as per forecast.

The inspired talk this time was that the regiment would be going south west from Guglionesi to Naples, where the big ship already in port, would be taking us to Blighty.

"But this Italian business isn't finished yet," muttered the scoffers, "we aren't even half way up the country - and you know the luck of this mob."

*Transfer to American Fifth Army, January 23rd, 1944.*

"They all say that," interjected one super cynic, "Alexander is more likely to be saying that we can be more usefully employed supporting the 78th Div., the 5th Div., or the 1st Canadian Div. - plus one or two Agras. "

"Prepare to move, prepare to move," was the bellowed order into the Troop position after we had fired a few rounds in support of 2nd Agra. As we usually slept in our gaiters and trousers we were on the ball and lined up in convoy order in time for the next order, "Mount. "

Hogmanay 1944 crept in at Carunchio on the Vasto-Castel di Sangro road with the usual lowering clouds and clinging misty rain. Our heads had been nudging the bottom layers of the rain clouds for days. So high and exposed were we on 1st January, 1944.

We leaguered in Battery order by the side of the road. The orders came thick and fast.

"You, you and you for guard," (luckily it didn't include me). There's four walls and a roof one hundred yards through the vineyard. Prepare to move 0.600 hrs. in the morning. Guard detail to report to Robert Freddy. Andiamo."

"Prepare to move at 0.600 hrs.?" I muttered. By now I was quite an expert in the undertone business. "Before that, if I know you. Just after we've hit the blanket, I bet.".

Charlie and I grabbed our bedding and hared it, as fast as our mid-thirties legs would allow, the hundred yards between the roadside and the barn.

"This all right, Tommaso". O.K. drop your blanket as a reserved card but don't go too far away. Blankets aren't reserved cards in absences. Shutters O.K.? It's mildish outside so with luck you never know. *Buono notte,* Tommaso. "

"*Buono notte,* Charlie". And then sheer exhaustion took over.

At four o'clock in the morning the scenery in the billet was unbelievable. Swirling snow had found the gaps in the window shutters, drifted in and given us all an extra blanket; of smooth soft snow. It was a very comfortable eiderdown until the search for socks, boots and trousers started. Numbed icy fingers were ready to drop off.

Wireless sets in Robert Freddy and George Freddy, parked in

33

convoy at the roadside were covered solid with snow where the elements, having found the gaps in the tarpaulins covering the tailboard, had seeped inside. Gun Quads were unrecognisable as such while Jeeps were buried out of sight.

At 7.15 in the morning there was another very heavy fall of snow which blocked the main road to Vasto. Although it was urgent that we move the next day, January 2nd, it was an impossible situation.

At ten minutes to two on the afternoon of the 2nd orders came to proceed towards Termoli via Vasto, on a transfer from 13 Corps front to 8th Army.

Whatever the Generals and the Brigadiers had proposed just then, in their chessboard moves of units, the winter weather in the Abruzzi took temporary control and foiled them. Snow fell blindly, icy gales ravaged the atmosphere and the river-beds became raging torrents, making life miserable and dreary.

We managed to move on January 4th; to San Martino, fifteen miles south-west of Ortona. When, for seven days we came to a full stop; snowed up again.

On January 11th a movement order was issued for us to proceed to Avellino, twenty miles east of Naples. After a regimental march of ninety five miles we arrived on the 12th.

On the 15th we moved to Corigliano in the Sessa Aurunca area, to play a supporting role in the crossing of the Garigliano river by the 5th (Yorkshire) Division.

"To the guns their thunder" made the night of January 16th 1944 a weary episode as every available man was put on detail to hump 25 pounder shells from the R.A.S.C. dumping point on the main road to the gun-position; a distance of about two hundred yards. A distance which increased as tiredness set in about midnight, as weary steps tottered down the goat-track.

As my strength went and I was slipping into Zombie-land, I muttered the motto of the Artillery, "Ubique, everywhere" and slumped into my bivvy at 4 o'clock in the morning.

The following day tragedy struck the regiment when Major Gallie and Capt. Hodges were killed by mines while recceing for Battery O.P's for the artillery barrage to be laid down for the river crossing.

Major Gallie was a fine Scotsman and Officer and I remembered him well from the first day I reported to the regiment at Dunblane, when he was Duty Officer.

Further casualties occurred in the minefield the following day, when there had been an attempt to recover the bodies.

The following day rumours of a promotion in the Signals Section to Lance Bombardier haunted Charlie and me. We were both quite content to remain on the bottom rung of the military ladder and we had no ambition to want higher. Our trade category of Gunner/Signaller/Driver/Operator while it had an imposing ring about it was nevertheless in the basement of the military establishment.

We heard that 'Doughy' thought that one of his George Freddy signallers was worthy of a stripe, to fill the vacancy caused by a Signals NCO going into hospital.

He must have been thinking more about our capabilities as truck cooks than about our technical knowledge of the guts of a number 22 wireless set. While I had a marvellous reputation as a concocter of good pancakes I hardly knew the difference between an ohm and a watt.

Good friends that we were we started pushing; I pushed for Charlie and Charlie pushed for me.

The sparring went something like this:- "Charlie, I hear that you're in line for a tape. The bush-wire is tapping it out fairly strongly that you've got a good chance. I'm doing my best for you, with Doughy."

"Tommaso, you've not been doing that behind my back? To think that I think you are a pal and all the time you're trying to promote me. You know stripes are not for me."

Before relations could get strained the regular incumbent came back from dock; before ponderous officialdom could appoint a substitute.

So we breathed a sigh of relief and resumed our normal carry-on.

Eventually we got rolling again.

South west it certainly was; to Blighty it certainly was not. The next map reference was for a place near Sessa Aurunca, where we humped twenty five pounder shells all night in preparation for a

35

barrage in support of the river crossing of the Garigliano by the 5th (Yorks) Div.

In the middle of January '44 the closely spaced postings of our mentor and friend Capt. (Doughy) Baker to 309 Battery and Bill

Queree, promoted to Lance Sergeant in Edward Troop, while we were in action near Sessa Aurunca on the Garigliano, halved the family of George Freddy.

George Freddy had been a happy truck ever since Baker, Queree, Harder and Roe had been established to it at Fyvie in the early days of July'42.

There had been 'encounters' of course. Which was inevitable when four men of different rank and varying temperaments were breathing down each others necks in battle, convoy and leaguer situations. But at the end of the day the score was level and the next day started off with zero marking.

Like the pages of a book, turning slowly from Introduction through to the Final Chapter the richly shared memories were marked as Experiences, capital E. Never to be forgotten.

We carried on with a new Gun Position Officer. A faceless Communist from Liverpool came as G.P.O. (Ack.), and contributed nothing to harmony on the truck. George Freddy was never the same again.

We were refreshed by the memories of the ups and downs of the last twenty months, when we had been cajoled and chivvied but never badgered by the best Gun Position Officer who ever worked out angles of sight and ranges for the guns.

And, as always, there was one particular memory that, somehow or other, lodged in the forefront of my mind; and that was the episode of the chicken.

As a roadside cook "Doughy" Baker had a tanner on himself as a male Mrs. Beeton. In Sicily, on the acquisition of a chicken - which was hardly superhuman considering that we were in a country populated by peasants and poultry - he decided that this challenged him to exhibit his culinary skill.

His second inspiration was that he would roast it in clay.

So we shovelled up some sandy soil, poured water over it and mixed it - to the same system as with mortar. Then the gallina - lacking head and feathers, of course - was rolled around in it and the repulsive yellow mud made a boundary around it.

It was then skewered up with a long prong and then slowly rotated over the glowing embers of a wood fire in the petrol tin container; the truck fireplace. The body of the doubtfully aged bird swung to and fro, over and under; the plaster cast baking solid.

Critical remarks flowed; Charlie looked at me, I looked at Charlie and Bill Querie looked at us both. Lifted eyebrows couldn't really be construed as "silent insubordination". Nevertheless it was a miracle that our Army Forms 252 - Charge Sheets - remained virgin.

We, the minions on his truck, had the collective disease of myopia. We never could see the pips of Authority on "Doughy's" epaulettes when we were in George Freddy four-man operation.

The twinkle in his eyes was his answer.

"Not going to plan, Sir?" I queried, after a while.

"Bit out of practice, Roe; early minutes yet, not to worry," he replied.

To myself, and to no others, I said "Sez you - and times not on your side. This is a mobile column and I'm sure Monty won't want to be held up by a slow chicken-roaster".

After a few minutes more the chef looked at his wrist watch and being Gun Position Officer with a knowledge of zero hours he decided that was it.

"Yes, I think she'll do," he said. "Looks good, don't you think, chaps."

We had no option but to agree, and the legs and the breast was shared out.

The result was a disaster. We spat out more dried clay than we chewed chicken.

"Actually", I muttered, "don't try it on us again."

Cheerio, Sir, and the very best of luck.

San Pietro, sheltering in the lea of the river Sangro and dominated by Monte Greco, 6,000 feet high, was our next battle area. We were supporting the 1st Canadian division in 13 Corps.

The village had been destroyed by enemy demolitions to deprive us of solid-walled winter quarters. Undulating piles of rubble, marking where the peasant cottages had been, formed one large mound of desolation. The heart-breaking sight indicated that the Germans had performed their demolition with Teutonic efficiency.

But oh, the tragedy that had come into the lives of innocent villagers by such a wanton outrage.

The noise of heavy explosions in the distance indicated that Borella and Gamberale were being given the same treatment.

We hadn't been in position long before two Messerschmitt 109's raced in at roof-top level and splayed cannon shells into the half demolished barn, but we were well to ground and the attack rolled over.

The coldness of the Abruzzi night seared our bones but the hospitality of the Canadian cooks with an ever-ready brew eased the misery somewhat. In the billets next to the cookhouse the only source of heating was from charcoal fires. We opted to huddle round the brazier and, with experience, moved away when our heads were being eased from our shoulders, on the way to the ceiling.

At the right moment we preferred a walk into the cold night air than to succumb to the toxic carbon monoxide fumes rising from the brazier.

To save a walk in the early hours of the morning there was a great demand from the cookhouse for empty tin cans to insert under the blanket. With practise we managed to avoid the jagged edges.

On the San Pietro position, for some unknown reason, there was a general issue of flour. So the truck cooks, rejects from the Army Catering Corps, had a chance to improve their culinary ability; which task up to now had only required a tin-opener.

Jam tarts, bully beef pies, cheese pies and pancakes saw the light of day from the improvised ovens and were downed with relish; just because they were different.

It was beyond human endeavour to mistreat flour over and above the capacity that was done at San Pietro, overlooking the Sangro.

The increased detail on sick parade two weeks later proved this point.

On December 21st we came out of action at San Pietro on the 1st Canadian Division front and moved across to Roccasicura for a rest, which had been well earned.

We were billeted in a peasant cottage, and we hoped we would be there for Christmas; and we were not disappointed.

The tidy living room, into which we were invited, enclosed shining pots and pans and a table worn through by constant scrubbing, showing devoted. care. Every nook and cranny was spotlessly clean.

Mama was middle-aged, if we judged correctly; and I think we did. Dressed in simple black, with no frills or furbelows, she knew no word of English but the way her eyes lit up when we entered the room indicated, full well, that the British strangers were welcomed to her modest hearth. And to share a hearth, however humble, with kindliness was a very, very acceptable thing to us just then when our thoughts at this season of Christmas, were winging away across the seas; to home.

We murdered the Italian language but, as always in this land, we got by. Miraculously - hand signals making up many deficiencies of the tongue - we eventually understood each other. And that was good.

The laboured conversations expressed for our part, that we appreciated not being thought of as foreign interlopers and, on mama's part, a happiness that her home was bringing some comfort into our lives.

To be awakened from sleep, on a hard stone floor, by the sound of the joyful pealing of church bells from the south - just across the valley - did me a power of good just then. As did the drone of bombers overhead, on their way to a mission against the Germans entrenched in the hills to the north.

On December 29th we kissed goodbye and moved east into action at Carrovilli on the Vasto road.

I knew that the implicit kindliness of the 'mama' living in the simple fashion that was her lot, would fashion a memory in my heart and that I would always remember the Christmas of 1943 in the tiny hill-village of Roccasicura, in the Apennines.

We were sent to a coastal sector position near Mondragane, just over the Garigliano, to relieve the 24th Field Regt., a unit of half-tracked guns.

It was a sandy position reminiscent of the desert except that the fine sand was held together by avenues of trees. Where, once again, sand infiltrated into messtins, made the digging of slit trenches twice as long and upset the cookhouse when "one round gunfire" was ordered.

About 9 o'clock in the evening we had been shelled but it had rolled over. The Command Post telephone rang and the GPO picked up the receiver and after establishing identity, listened.

It was an enquiry from Edward Troop if we could send a stretcher across as they had a casualty.

So I clicked for the job.

Everything was stacked against me. It was a very dark night, with not a star in the sky, I had a weighty burden and the avenue of trees cancelled out nearly every vestige of orientation to a gun position in a location for which I had only a rough bearing. I chewed sand twice when I went to ground in a hurry.

To this day I cannot explain how I got to Edward Troop. But the important thing, I delivered the stretcher and set off on the return journey; with a big problem on my mind. How to get back.

By a combination of intuition and good luck I made it.

"Manage it, Roe?" the GPO enquired, through half-shut eyes.

"Yes sir." I replied.

"Good show." Heavy breathing allied to the brevity of the conversation from the officer indicated that my anticipation of a recommendation for a medal had been a misplaced one.

Exhausted by the trudge, I was in a nasty mood. "I hope you get a good dollop of gritty sand in your M & V tomorrow," I muttered as I settled down to Command Post duty again.

I wasn't in any better mood the following day when a typhus inoculation parade turned up; my ninth inoculation altogether and the third in the month of January 1944. Captain Nash, a likeable Canadian, who had joined us at Paoli was our Medical Officer.

Sleeves rolled up, we got into line. As we moved slowly forwards toward the needle our ears were cocked for the sound of enemy firing from the area of Minturno, on the north side of the Gariglione from where German artillery had been active for a few days.

Doc. Nash had made six jabs when the all too familiar sounds of phee-ew, phee-ew, boomp, boomp ruffled the atmosphere. We all hit the ground, face downwards. The taste of the gritty sand as we burrowed down was familiar but still repulsive.

Familiarity had not improved the taste.

Luckily the shells, spewing up the earth, landed a hundred yards short.

As the little stonk dried up, shaken, we resumed the trudge forward; to ensure another entry under the heading 'Protective Inoculations', on page nine of the Pay Book.

We did what was asked of us and then for the next few days we edged our way south east, away from events.

We arrived at a place called Murano di Napoli, in the suburbs of Naples; as the name implies. This leaguer area, almost in sight of the funnels of the big ships in the port, revitalised the grape-vine and the Blighty story got off the ground with renewed vigour, again.

Little did we know, on 1st February 1944, that what happened in the next fourteen weeks would rank as an important entry in the curriculum of the military historians of the future.

Preliminary orders came through, preparing us to embark with 168 Infantry Brigade.

The following day, after the ritual M and V mess-tin splash, the traditional opening gambit in Royal Artillery Order of March Procedure - "Mount" - which we knew off by heart - came down the line.

The Battery vehicles formed up and at 3.45 p.m. George Freddy moved out from the farmyard and moved to the Regimental start point at the fork roads linking Marano with Mugnano.

In regimental convoy we travelled to Pozzuoli where embarkation on LST's Y005 and Y006 started at 9 p.m.

For the umpteenth time we were on our way to an unknown destination.

In action, which seemed to be more often than not, most destinations were unknown to the O.R.s. Oh, you could look up at the sun in the sky to locate direction, work out the running time from where you knew you had just left and have a guess; but the winding roads and side tracks threw you. So, from a factual point of view you were wasting your time. As a mind occupier, though, the conjecture was rewarding.

Only the important people, the officers and the gentlemen, with their maps and coloured pencils knew, roughly, their next location. Whether it was padrone Guiseppi Martelli's vineyard four miles north west or Tommaso Locatini's olive grove five miles north east for a suitable gun position even the important people did not know exactly until the contours of the land had been reccied for good cover.

So long as the direction 'north' appeared in the movement orders that omission was alright by me. I knew Derbyshire was still basically north and any trek, short or long, in that direction was my heartfelt wish.

So we waved goodbye to Naples, to the big ships in the port and to the Blighty hopes; proving once again that rumours couldn't be relied on.

# CHAPTER THREE

### Anzio Beachhead.

We set sail on the evening of 2nd February and after an uneventful voyage northwards along the Tyrrhenean coastline arrived at the entrance to Hell; a little port called Anzio, thirty five miles south of Rome.

The ramps of the LST's lowered slowly on to the jetty and the wireless trucks, the Quads towing the twenty five pounders, the Monkey trucks for the line signallers and the "soft" vehicles nosed out from the cavernous belly of the ship and turned right on to the narrow dockside road.

We were on our way to help out against the expected German counter-attack against the 1st British (Infantry) Div. and the American VI Corps who had landed some days previously.

We soon realised we had Germans to the north, Germans to the west and Germans to the east with the Tyrrhenean Sea at our backs. It was a chilling thought.

"Get moving, get moving" yelled the burly corporal of the Military Police, directing the traffic at the junction of the access road from the jetty, where in peaceful times, the shops and pensiones had catered for the Roman holiday-makers.

He jabbed his thumb over his right shoulder and we knew, loud and clear, through his words and his actions which direction we had to take; away from the port area *presto*; "there's no time to picnic here", he bellowed "you'll soon find that out. Move, move."

We heeded the advice from his beachhead experience and moved; fast.

The gaunt shells of the shattered buildings in the dock area formed a grim back-cloth. The tottering brick skeletons with their girder ribs exposed criss-cross were spewed around in disarray.

The sight of the devastation around the jetty and the drone of planes in the sky above was the whiplash to jog life into George Freddy and the rest of the regimental convoy.

February 3rd was a miserable day; on all counts. It was cold

*Anzio port area*

with leaden skies hung with heavy clouds. All the hurry and bustle indicated that 168 Brigade was urgently needed to plug a gap in the front line. The London Scottish were thrown in immediately.

It appeared to me that the 78th Field, being either Corps artillery or Agra artillery, was always on tap to be slung anywhere on a one hundred and fifty miles wide sector, from the Adriatic to the Tyrrhenian Sea.

Past history proved my point; Gabes (Tunisia) 10 Corps, Takrouna, 5th Agra, Reggio di Calabria, 6th Agra, Rionero, 13 Corps, Sessa Aurunca, 2nd Agra - plus the supporting of at least seven divisions.

I reckoned that the amount of leave given in our mob was the lowest of anybody in the Allied Armies. It appeared that there was a permanent hot-line to the 78th Field.

In the first hours we had our first casualties.

Since debouching from LST 7005, regimental transport had shuttled backwards and forwards from the port to the gun position with stores and ammunition and there was a feverish digging of slit trenches and Command Posts.

At about midnight two drivers, Alfie Flear and McLellan, returned to base to get some rest after a harrassing day.

It proved to be their last day on earth.

News came the following morning that they had been killed by butterfly bombs thrown out by German Bombers.

Too tired to dig for protection - exhaustion dictating their actions - they had decided to sleep in their vehicles.

So, within hours, we had our first casualties.

Even at that early stage, piecing the Sitreps together, it looked as if we had arrived with 168 Brigade, just in time to defend the beachhead against the first real enemy counter-attack since the landing. The Germans had been given the chance to bring reinforcements down from the north. Their purpose was to nip out the salient which had failed to reach Campoleone on the 1st Division front and Cisterna on the American eastern sector.

The 3rd Infantry Brigade, comprising the Sherwood Foresters, Kings Own Shropshire Light Infantry and the Duke of Wellington's Regiment were having a terrible time and gradually being pushed back.

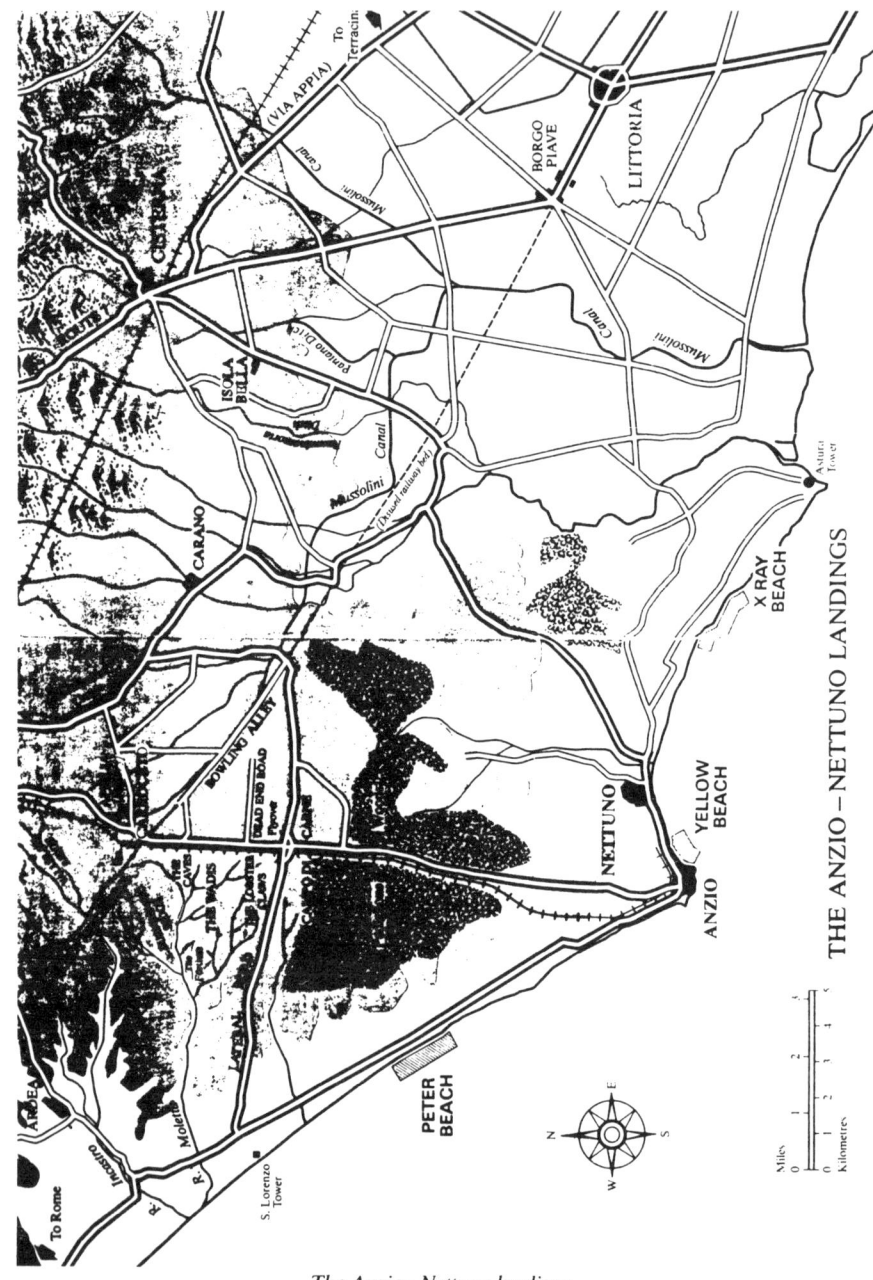

*The Anzio - Nettuno landings.*

February 3rd hadn't a single redeeming feature - except the comradeship, which had been amongst us since Alamein - and when the enemy artillery ceased at three o'clock on the morning of the 4th, after a four-hour barrage, I had had enough. And it was only the first day.

What with the harassing fire of the German artillery, the bombing, the butterfly bombs and the foul weather the first forty eight hours were pretty miserable.

Our first deployment area had been by the side of a hard-metalled, secondary, road but point 8521 was too easily spotted by the German planes patrolling overhead so we moved out in a hurry to the shelter of point 8427, a portion of the Campagna hard by Campo Circus in the Padiglione Woods, which had been earmarked for the gun positions. This information added nothing in detail to my military knowledge. All I knew was that I was still in Italy, that I was a long long way from home, and that furthermore, it looked as if I was destined to be in Italy for a good while yet.

Provided that one didn't arrive with my name and number on it.

First thoughts are not always deep thoughts and so on reflection, I made an amendment on the last bit. If one did arrive with my name and number on it, my duration in this bit of Italy would be a much longer one.

I cheered myself up by calculating that at that moment of time, 3rd February, 1944, 1 had roughly halved the distance from El Alamein to my own doorstep in Derbyshire. Then settled down to what turned out to be a very long acquaintanceship with the undergrowth trees and subsoil of the Padiglione woods; close by a forlorn piece of railway embankment compulsorily acquired from the Ferrovie dello Stato and about to achieve as the 'Flyover' the reputation of being one of the most dreaded spots on the beachhead; indeed in the whole war.

Our first orders were to dig and dig deep and reading the signs of real war, we dug and kept digging. Shovels literally shed sparks as subsoil followed topsoil. I marvelled how many thousand shovelfuls of earth had to be thrown upwards to make a reasonable hole in the ground for a Command Post.

Although ostensibly attached to the 1st. Infantry Div. at 4th

February, we engaged targets on all sectors. On a packed beachhead with a perimeter ten miles by eight miles and a situation leading up to a build-up of enemy forces - in preparation for a major attack down the Albano/Anzio road - our first days were harassing. The daily expenditure of ammunition was close to exceeding the supply. Nevertheless, 456 Battery guns - with our sister Batteries 309 and 310-battered away at the reported targets.

I had a gut feeling that 5th February was not going to be an entry in my Happy Calendar for 1944 and so it proved; I got a detail as Signaller in the relieving party for the Flyover OP; this detail not unexpected was my first at this notorious landmark. Its reputation as a trouble spot had filtered through to us on our first shovellings out for the foxholes.

As dusk set in we prepared to move out from the shelter of the woods. Geared up with freshly charged Dags for the wireless set, rations for the two day stint and other spares, we clambered aboard the armoured car, moved slowly along the rutted cart-track and tentatively approached the junction with the main Albano Road. Appropriately named "Stragglers Post". Which interpreted, for the uninitiated, said - in effect - "If you are going north, watch out and step on the gas".

German guns had this section of the main road well registered in their Fire Plan.

Turning left the driver hustled through the gear box, to get into top gear and we hared along the Albano Road. I inwardly prayed that German fingers were not hovering restlessly on their gun triggers. The tension of the journey dried up the small talk and we each withdrew into our innermost shells. We sped along the Albano Road.

The distance seemed interminable but at last the vague outline of the Flyover bridge appeared out of the blackness of the night. The driver of the armoured car appeared to have suffered the agony of the Stragglers Post - Flyover run before as, without prompting, he turned left on to a rutty cart-track on the south side of the embankment, proceeded about fifty yards and then stopped. An abandoned Sherman tank was a marker for the entrance to the OP in the embankment, a forlorn reminder of past activity.

Battle noises rumbled in the near distance as we disembarked from the armoured car. Fumbling hands gathered kit and wireless spares together. So there we were for forty-eight hours.

"Right," said the Lieutenant in charge, "Either of you two been up here before?"

"No, Sir," was the emphatic reply.

"'O.K., that makes three of us."

We eased ourselves into the narrow tunnel; it was just wide enough for two thin ones to pass; sideways.

"We're reporting to the 2nd Sherwood Forester H.Q for liaison" said the Lieutenant.

We started out as a party of three but we had not gone far, when for some inexplicable reason the officer changed his mind and instructed me to go back to the tunnel and stay put. They vanished into the night.

I was alone in my lonely world. The screeching and whining of shells coming and going, made me realise that, after the diving Stukas at El Alamein, this was my closest acquaintanceship with real war. The noisy suspicions of the horrible night increased the distance between the open scrub-land and the OP under the cover of the embankment. Verey lights illuminated the area and I froze into the landscape. Only. on the wane, did I resume my half-crouching stumbling walk. The knowledge that Germans were on the prowl to the north, to the east, and to the west made me the loneliest of men.

If anyone, just then, had accused me of being very frightened they would have been dead right.

How I did it I can never explain, but luck was with me and I arrived back at the tunnel OP and flopped inside. In the security of that little tunnel, scooped out of the dirt and ashes of the railway embankment by the Royal Engineers, my guts returned to their rightful place and I breathed again. I still lived in hopes that the Lieutenant and my wireless mate would return.

The narrow, eighteen inch wide tunnel was shored up by supporting timbers. Through the roof dirty water seeped by the slow-dripping gallon down my neck, pit-a-pat, pit-a-pat. A box up-ended, was the only piece of furniture to sit on; but it was a home of sorts.

To bolster my courage I tried a soft whistle but far from having a soothing effect it turned sour on me. I never could whistle in tune. I remembered, belatedly, that even a soft whistle in an enclosed space always seems to shriek out. My mind, a welter of imagination, led me to think that the mixed up melody of musical notes would attract the attention of a roving Jerry patrol to my hideout.

But I wanted some noise to keep me sane. Locked as I was, a captive in my solitude. My toe tapped out a soft evenbeat exercise against the timber sidesupport against which I was straddled. At every slight turn to easy my body, my scraggy knees scraped against the shoring timbers of the miserable gallery. The dripping water treatment continued right through the night.

Hour after hour passed in a slow sequence. Although the battle noises around Campoleone were muted I hated every minute of that dreadful night.

At about four o'clock a working party from the Royal Engineers appeared in the entrance to the tunnel and my long, lonely, and what seemed pointless, vigil was over. It was the only occasion in my whole Army career that I felt tempted to kiss a Sergeant of H.M. Forces. My relief was as heartfelt as that.

I was determined, if it was humanly possible, to contact my kid brother, Bernard, who was with the 2nd Bn. Sherwood Foresters, on the original landing. The coloured chinograph pencil marks on the Command Post maps showed the 2nd Foresters in the southern Padiglione woods, nearer the port, and on the right hand side of the main Anzio road. Any talk of Rest Area at Anzio was merely a clinging to Army terminology, not a single square yard of the beachhead was restful. There were no safe places.

Wanting to get in touch with him as soon as I could, if I had to comb the woods, I set out on a voyage of discovery. I reckoned that we were about a mile apart the distance from our gun position along the via Anziate, and then off right into the southern woods. So I set off and eventually got to Bedford Street- obviously not an original Italian Strada. An enquiry or two later and I was directed by the lads of the Duke of Wellington's Regt. to the Foresters area. It was the 3rd Infantry Brigade area.

Our first meeting was joyous and momentous; an infantryman of the regular Army with staging posts from 1930 onwards at

50

Multan in India, Khartoum in the Sudan, Guernsey in the Channel Islands etc. etc. before the war had a lot to say to a Gunner/ Signaller in the Royal Artillery about family, about events since they landed in North Africa with the 1st Army and about future hopes. The elder brother, the Signaller, also had a lot of catching up to do.

My feelings in turmoil, matched the pouring rain erupting from the lowering skies. Dusk, setting in, increased the sombre setting. An infantry C. Q. M. S. hasn't much time on his hands when his Company is in front of the Flyover so the family talk had to be of the shortest of durations. The ration train for 'B' Company was imperative and at dusk he would be going forward with the supplies. I wished him luck and asked for the use of his dugout for the night. His was better covered than mine and the tempting thought of his well sandbagged hole easily pushed aside the nagging thought of being charged as a deserter from my Troop. With Germans all around us and the sea at our backs, where could I have deserted to, anyway?

The matter was clinched when I thought of my own inadequately covered rabbit warren.

As dusk dropped its curtain of uncertainty I stood back in the obscurity of the overhanging trees; a bystander in the briefing of the battlekitted Sherwoods, getting ready for a move out from Padiglione to the front line at the Factory and Buono Riposo ridge.

They knew by what had gone on since the landing that there would be no morrow for some of them but the light chatter thrust the thought to the back of their minds.

The bystanding share I had of the occasion froze my blood and lived with me. I was thankful to be Artillery.

They moved out and I went to Bernard's dugout, to do the best I could to get some rest. The night, as usual, was interminable. Strange circumstances in strange surroundings made me all the more restless.

About four o'clock in the morning, well before the first rays of dawn had begun to lighten the skies, the dejected figure of my kid brother flopped wearily into the dugout.

I didn't need to be told that death had stalked freely that night,

February 8th, 1944 was a tragic and heroic night for the 2nd Sherwood Foresters.

With a heavy heart I said cheerio and hitched a lift back to Campo Circus and George Freddy gun position. My luck was in and I was in time for my next stint at the controls of the wireless set, with Fire Orders supporting the 1st Div.; and any others who wanted it.

On the morrow, my monkey-on-a-tree mental set-up, where irrelevant thoughts swung from branch to branch - which was my normal temperament but which had been accentuated already by knowing Anzio - caused me to ask myself a question. "I wonder how Bedford Street, the Sherwood Foresters rest area (joke, there was no rest area anywhere) got its name?"

"Bedford Street" on the Southern end of the western side of Via Anziate, in Padiglione woods was really San Anastasia.

I pondered on this for a few moments, and the next question which popped up was something like this; "Is there a Bedfordshire regiment on the Beachhead?"

I couldn't remember one from the location pins on the Command Post Sitrep maps.

"Shropshire    Light Infantry; no link there; Duke of Wellingtons Regiment, no link there; Sherwood Foresters, no link there, either. The counties are all miles away from Bedford ... Oh, a last thought on the subject. Could it be the name of the Commander of the 3rd Infantry Brigade ... Hum, why do I think about such a trivial thing just now? Does it matter, does it really matter how it was named?"

A few minutes on I gave myself the benefit of a piece of self-inflicted philosophy. I informed myself that while I had been trying to sort out the riddle of Bedford Street my mind had taken a beneficial diversion from the serious thing in a gun position.

Brief though it was, the experience was good for me. But Bedford Street remained an unsolved riddle. I welcomed the mental exercise but I would have liked an answer.

On the evening of February 9th I got my second detail to the Flyover OP.

"Getting too frequent for my peace of mind," I thought "but I guess they know a good signaller when they see one" my in-built propaganda department enlightened me, trying to cheer me up.

We turned right off the Albano road, went parallel with the Flyover embankment, bumped along the track and stopped at the entrance to the Observation Post; or OP to us.

Gathering my kit together I prepared to rush the embankment, to reach the shelter of the little cubby-hole sized haven of security on the south side.

As I scrambled up the scrabbly embankment my mind was on the churn; the mental relief at being near to safety being submerged by the fear of what might happen before I got inside. In the inky black darkness of the rainy night my eyes were wide open for the comer. My state of mind had not been helped by the news that there had been five casualties in the regiment that day.

That embankment, seemed like a mountain-side as I edged two steps forward and slid one step backwards in the mud. Progress on the greasy slope of cloying mud was painfully slow.

From 5 o'clock on the following morning I was fully employed and my ears got flatter and flatter and got a closer relationship with my cheeks. The wireless headphones had little chance to be pushed off, as two hundred guns battered away at tank targets and assembling German infantry near Carroceto station; threatening the Scots Guards in a vital sector just in front of the Flyover.

Peering through the O.P. slitty, in the embankment, for observation of enemy movement the binoculars opened out on open desolate, scrub-land. We knew it was interlaced with wadis known as Lobster Claw, Oh God Wadi and The Boot but there was no sign of movement in front of the Flyover. But we knew that hundreds of courageous infantrymen were holed up in these wadis, in the rain rapidly becoming waterways. No shelter from the elements lying up in daylight - not daring to move above ground-constantly harassed by German shellfire, mortaring and small arms fire these brave men looked death in the face many times.

The sight of an infantryman coming out of the front line filled me, a lucky gunner/signaller, with admiration and pride. And I muttered to myself "Thank God I'm in the Artillery and not the Infantry. "

Every man jack of them deserved a medal as big as a frying pan and every infantry battalion a special citation.

*Anzio No. 3 dug-out row*

*Anzio flyover bridge - final defence line*

The railway line went northwards, in a straight line to Carroceto station, and beyond, to enemy occupied country. The Albano road ran parallel with it and on either side of the road small trees, defoliated by the rigours of winter and enemy gunfire, stood out like evenly spaced sentinels. The electric pylons and the small cluster of deserted buildings of the station, slap bang in the middle of the battle area, were forlorn reminders of happier days for the *Ferrovie dello Stato*.

In the dim recesses of my mind, linked with my seventeen years of seniority with the London and North Eastern Railway Company, I began conjecturing on daft things. At least afterwards, away from the scene, they seemed daft but I reckoned it was a healthy state to have thoughts; especially unshackled ones, in our circumstances.

"Where did the people of Carroceto go, when they boarded a train? To Anzio, for a day at the seaside or to Rome for shopping and sight-seeing?

"Did the Station Master live in a Station House, on the premises, as they do in Britain?"

No doubt, once again Mr. Freud would be able to give detailed reasons for the odd workings of my mind at this particular moment of time.

Looking through the peephole at Carroceto I thought - with the bit that the Army hadn't squashed out of existence with its'Yes, Sir; No, Sir'cult.

"It'll really be Carroceto, the insignificant country railway station on the Rome/Anzio line, peopled - before 1944 - with peasant sheep farmers, Aprilia, the Factory and the territory in front of the Flyover bridge that will be the landmarks in the memories of those poor buggers in the infantry, slipping and sliding in the mud of the wadis; often too exhausted to get out of the trench, when the name Anzio 1944 is marked on the map of 'Historic Battles'.

Think of El Alamein; where it all started. Perched on a sea of sand was a shed, passing as a railway station; where at home you wouldn't have kept your homing pigeons. That is, if you kept pigeons.

Funny, I've only just cottoned on that I'm talking about two railway stations, separated by about two thousand miles.

So what happens?

Alamein will be recorded as the place where our disasters stopped and victories started coming ... By the way, to prove the point, do you realise that we haven't been in a retreat yet?" I seemed to be talking as if I had other company. In reality I was talking to myself. "Strange, isn't it, how often little unknown places become battle landmarks."

On February 10th fifteen German tanks were reported around the Factory; the name given to Aprilia, the Model Village - Mussolini's showpiece - between Carroceto and Campoleone.

The weather was so bad that the Air Force was grounded. So two hundred guns were zeroed onto one of the most feared locations in the whole beachhead. The Factory was always in the centre of the action.

The following day the rain pelted down and turned the terrain into clinging slush. The damp seeped into our bones and into our bedding. When the atmospherical conditions carved out a clause in the descriptive phrase "Sunny Italy. " Giving the impression - before we knew better that there was nothing but sunshine and blue skies in the land of spaghetti and ice cream. We knew different, after clambering along the spiny backbone of Italy.

The entries in the 'Weather' column of the Troop Log in our first week said it all, with dreary daily entries of "Heavy rain" -"Cloudy, rain" - Overcast, slight drizzle". Certainly a baptism with plenty of the main ingredient; water.

On 11th February a personal message from Major General Penney, Commanding the British 1st Div., was published to all ranks.

"In forwarding the attached copy of a message from the Commander VI U.S. Corps I can only add my expression of utmost admiration of the way in which the 1st Div. including its attached units and formations, both British and American has met all demands on it.

I would remind you all of the words in which the great Admiral Drake prayed before the battle of Cadiz nearly 500 years ago

"O Lord God when thou givest to thy servants to endeavour any great matter, grant us also to know that it is not the beginning but the continuing of the same until it is thoroughly finished which fielded the true Glory . "

You will all, I know, meet every demand that may be made on you with the same determination and spirit which has characterised the performance of those gallant men who have suffered wounds, capture or death on the performance of their duty to the Allied cause. Remember our debt to them.

You have inflicted grievous loss on the enemy. Stick to it and look forward to the day when we shall again be on the march. "

"End of text and pull your chest in", I thought "I've heard it all before. It bears a great resemblance to Monty's "knock'em for six" order in the Western Desert, just before Alamein. Amen to all that, particularly the last fourteen words.

Charlie had been in the front row in the Ear, Nose and Throat department when the original issue had been made; his ears missed nothing, his nose smelled out everything and his tongue, while having a sarcastic touch, had a witty twinge to it. A kind of revised version of the three wise monkeys all rolled into one Army number.

"Tommaso, what's that little book you keep writing in, from time to time; or to put it more clearly, on a regular spasmodic system. "

"Little book, Carlo. What little book?"

I could afford to act simple because when he started the ball rolling with his first question I was not actually caught in the act.

"Oh, you mean my War Diary." I replied.

"Yes if your little private book is your War Diary that is what I mean." said Carlo. "A War Diary for a Gunner/Signaller/Driver/ Operator, one of the lower echelons of the Royal Artillery, if I may say so, is thinking big from a small base," quipped my lanky friend from Burseldon.

In the back of the 14 cwt. wireless truck, too lanky for me when his kneecaps beat a tattoo on my vertebrae as we reccied the rough cart tracks for suitable gun positions.

This time we were at ease sitting on the edge of my dug-out exchanging news from home.

Our ears were on 'Stand To' for the noise of the 'comers'. The date, I thought, was 12th February but I wasn't quite sure as calendars were not that plentiful.

Taking a hefty suck at his blackened pipe - which was overdue to be pensioned off - a pipe which had emitted various obnoxious fumes on the way from Alamein - the supply source being described as from camel dung (from which Victory V cigarettes were also alleged to have originated) a reply was obviously being manufactured.

Having nothing to enlarge on at that stage, I allowed him freedom of speech, which was fair, as it was supposed to be one of the attributes of the civilisation we were fighting for.

There was one exclusion clause. Kings Regulations did not cater for too much freedom of speech from the bottom rung of the Establishment to the Sergeants, Sergeant Majors, Lieutenants and officers upwards.

Charlie, never the one to ease up, came charging in again. "What do you want a War Diary for anyway? Fancy yourself as a historian? Against Regimental Orders isn't it? Hoping to get famous some day? The question marks were running out of supply, so thick and fast did the questions come.

"Don't you forget it, my lad," (there was only a year between us) you won't go down to posterity from your memoirs. No publisher will want to know. There'll be a great big queue of Field Marshalls, Admirals, Air Marshalls, Generals and Brigadiers a mile long outside their offices. All presenting their version of war history in various guises. Covering up their mistakes by classifying it as strategy and their lack of initiative, at the time it was needed, as consolidation. The officers and the gentlemen will have a good run with their memoirs. And I'll tell you something else; their individual interpretations of the same bit of action will differ. The privates and the gunners on ground-floor level will be among the also-rans. "

"Let there be no mis-understanding, Carlo - which there should not be between buddies - at the end of it all, if we are lucky enough to get out alive to repossess a National Insurance number and, worse, an Inland Revenue Tax Reference I shall reap a sort of warm feeling when I turn the pages of my war diary. As the demob suit will be the last piece of equipment issued to you by an Army Quartermaster it will be a dead cert. it won't fit you. Any bets? Anyway we've wandered off the subject. Let me read you one or two extracts from the little book you're so nosy about. "

April 23rd 1943 - Still in action ... on the plains below Tacrouna. "Jerry" annoyed us by throwing a few back. Supported the Free French.
On the way to Kairouan linked up with the first American troops from 1st Army. Divebombed on road, by Messerschmitts. I dived into a 12 foot cactus bush for cover. Darning needles are very painful when embedded in one's stomach. "You can vouch for that, you helped to pluck some out."
May 13th Moved to Sfax. Training between 13th and 25th. On 25th went to Rest Camp at Mahdia on the coast for five days. On a day trip to Monastir located the whereabouts of Bernard's unit, the 2nd Sherwood Foresters - at Sousse. Next day, cadging a lift and with CO's authority, set out to find him. Saw the Foresters flag flying just outside Sousse. A memorable day when 8th Army met 1st Army. Returned to Mahdia by Foresters
transport.
July 21st Preparing for Sicily. Marched (crawled would be a better word) I 1/2miles in the midday sun with full kit expecting to go over to Sicily, but departure put back."

"So you see, Charles, there's no court martial material there as it was past history when pencil hit the paper. 'Capito'?"

"No comments, Tommaso. You've got a good point."

"Charlie", I said "pardon the pun, but I know the drill. These personal notes will always be tucked away at the bottom of my kitbag. And as you know kitbags are never inspected. Contents of, yes. Kitbags, no. When this lot's over if fate decrees that I am due for a Civvy Suit at a Demob Centre I shall want to look back at my own bit of history-making. Don't you forget it mate, there have been occasions when my speed and accuracy at the controls of the George Freddy wireless set has either helped our infantry boys up

59

forward or has stopped a Jerry attack. That goes for you too. That thought is in my mind because I know I won't be gazetted, or whatever they call it when you get a medal. I'm fated to do my feats of valour incognito and unsung, or under cover of darkness when there is no recommending officer within six miles. OK Charlie, point taken."

I took a deep breath, which I needed badly after that lengthy speech, sighed and crept away.

Making sure that my little book and a pencil were put in a place ready for the next interesting item.

On February 12th almost before the words were out of my mouth, another commendatory letter was pushed through the Regimental letter box; this time from Lieut-General R. L. McCreery, Commanding 10 Corps.

"It is now ten months since you joined 10 Corps at Enfidaville. During that time you have shown fighting qualities-in Tunisia, across the broad plains of Naples, on Monte Camino and recently during the victorious assault across the River Garigliano.

This is a great record. I am very proud of you and thank you all for your loyalty and unfailing courage.

The time has come for you to undertake a fresh task away from 10 Corps but I sincerely hope we shall be together again. All good luck and every success in the work that lies ahead.

10 Corps will watch your progress eagerly and our thoughts will always be with you in the days to come. "

So without wanting to detract from the kindly sentiments expressed in the letter from Major General Penney, Commander of the 1st Div. and Lieut. General R. L. McCreery, Commander of 10 Corps but, by now, being pretty adept at interpreting straws in the wind I said to myself, "something's going to happen. "

So I got the truck shovel, dug deeper and looked for more tree trunks to put on top of the dug-out.

Just in case.

And we only had four days before we found out.

February 16th was ushered in by engaging targets at map reference 897352. Then ominous reports came through (although unconfirmed) that twenty enemy tanks had been seen at map reference 875347.

At six o'clock on the morning of 16th February a terrific German artillery barrage broke out. The Command Post was a hive of industry as message after message came in and Fire Order followed Fire Order in quick succession as the enemy targets were pinpointed by the O.P.'s.

The German attacks seemed to be coming from all quarters and with weight.

Being a signaller on duty at the Command Post meant that you got the news hot from the press, so to speak. Feelings became taut as information came in at nine o'clock that German tanks, supported by massive formation of infantry were rumbling south on the Albano road and were reported in the Carroceto area.

It looked as if the big attack to drive us back into the sea was under way.

At nine o'clock twenty three enemy tanks, in groups of three and four, and massed infantry were reported at map reference 892334. An hour later six MK VI tanks were reported to be moving south east.

Without let-up our guns attacked reported targets and U targets were fired at 12 o'clock, 12.45 hrs., 13.10, 13.15, 14.15 and 15.45 hrs.

"Roey, Roey; Wakey Wakey, your turn now. It's 2 o'clock OK?" The voice of Johhny Fulton the signaller on duty in the Command Post filtered down the steps of my dugout, and circled round with the clarity that resounds when unease is present. As it always was at Anzio. Johnny was a good guy; guaranteed to give 101 per cent at all times. An Englishman to be proud of.

"OK, Johnny. I'll be there in a minute or two. "

The good old Nostell Priory squaddy days of changing from PT kit to full battledress in three minutes dead (and woe betide you if your braces got entangled or your buttons just wouldn't button) meant that my bits and pieces were ready to hand. I didn't have to bother about my pyjama trousers - I had slept in them. They were khaki coloured and scratchy to the skin.

A million thoughts in an untidy tangle churned through my mind as I reached for my steel helmet and padded between the scruffy bushes towards the Command Post.

Johnny Fulton went on his way, thankfully, to No. 4 Dugout Row. The undesirable residence, with a leaky roof, under the drip, drip of the rainfall sliding down the leaves of the oak trees in Padiglione Woods.

The only company I had was the heavy breathing of the G.P.O., trying to snatch a few winks of sleep after a harassing day.

My feet dangling in a thin skin of floor water, tin hat at the ready and a humming wireless set, that was more the harbinger of disaster than of comfort, added their ingredients towards a tense night. A night we guessed that Jerry was probing in depth, in preparation for a big attack to push us all back into the sea, from whence we had come.

At three o'clock in the morning, when even in normal times the strength of civilisation is at its lowest ebb, a dug-out approximately twelve square yards in acreage in a wooded area in the middle of a surrounded beachhead was a hellish spot to be in. With butterfly bombs shovelled out from German planes, enemy shelling directed from the Alban Hills and a possible earthquake from the 280 mm 'Anzio Annie,' firing from the end of the railway tunnel all adding their regular contributions to the cacophony of battle.

A brooding air of stalking death covered the Roman Campagna as the grumbles of death and destruction rolled in the northern distance.

On the 17th February the dawn ventured in cold, cheerless and devoid of high expectations. The feverish pattern of the previous day continued, and warned us to expect more trouble. One of the first reports came from 309 Battery, who reported that seven German tanks and 300 infantry were preparing to attack down the Albano road.

At 8.45 we fired a Murder concentration at map reference 897365 where enemy gun flashes had been spotted. At 9.52 German tanks were reported moving south.

Fire Orders ripped the atmosphere apart as the enemy pressure was sustained. At 16.04 hrs. enemy tanks were reported in great numbers at map reference 859313. Fifteen minutes later 309 Battery reported ten German tanks at map reference 863305.

At 16.40 hrs. our O.P. was asked if they could confirm that enemy tanks were 300 yards north of the Flyover. Which meant they were near our final beachhead line.

The sight of the Troops guns firing on an angle east north east (a signaller's interpretation, not a gunners) was a jolting sight.

"What's going off, Don?" I asked. Don Humphries was the gun sergeant on the nearest gun. "Things look tricky to me, the direction the gun spouts are pointing."

Don Humphries was another Sassenach in a Scottish mob, hailing from near the sound of Bow Bells. I had always remembered his patient exposition on astrology as we approached Capetown in the Empress of Japan troopship on llth August, 1942; when he pointed out the location of Cassiopeá in the firmament on a clear star-studded night.

Another nice guy Sergeant.

Although, as a wireless operator, I was unversed in the technical side of gunnery my knowledge of angles of sight and range was enough to tell me that when all Freddy Troops guns were firing on an angle of sight of 70 degrees and all at once at a much shorter range, things were hotting up.

Don's reply was forceful and to the point.

"It's sticky, very sticky," he said. Jerry's putting in everthing he's got in this attack. Just get your gym shoes to the top of your kit bag, you might want them sharpish.

Just then the order "three rounds gunfire" came through so Don Humphries did not hear my reply. But I went away to do as he said.

The battle raged right through the day and continued into the 18th. It was a day of deep personal tragedy; a day I shall never forget.

When I had been relieved from the Command Post duty in the very early hours of the morning I said "No breakfast for me, this time I'm staying below ground to catch up on some kip. "

About seven a.m. the mixed sound of voices and feverish activity crept down my dug-out steps and lodged themselves into my hazy existence. Years of two hours on and four off meant-to me at least - that I was never far away from reality, even when allegedly sleeping. Throwing on my battledress blouse I clambered out of my dug-out.

"What's happened, what's happened, anybody hit?" I asked.

"Yes," said Sergeant Davis of number 3 gun. "Fred, your mate's been killed. Thought it was you at first. Then somebody remembered you had said you were staying below. A Jerry shell hit a tree and showered shrapnel down. Dickinson, the G.P.O. Ack. got some shrapnel through his back; he's in a bad way, Taffy Watkin got some shrapnel in his shoulder blade. He should be OK."

The tragic news that Fred was dead just would not sink in to my numbed mind. "Oh, no. Why must good blokes die. Why, why, why?"

It was a heartbreaking experience to sit in the back of a 15 cwt. truck with the body of your buddy wrapped in a blanket on the way to the burial ground on the hillside overlooking the port.

The harsh clattering of a shovel as it was forced out of my hands as we passed over a bumpy bit of the cart-track, on our way to the burial ground on the western slope overlooking the port, added a deep poignancy to the occasion.

My mind, a welter of uncontrolled thoughts, wandered back higgledy-piggledy, to the good times and the bad times shared in the last year with the blanket-covered figure, lying on the floor of the truck, between two pairs of Army boots.

Silence reigned as shovels plied a gradual way through the topsoil. Our hearts were too heavy to want words.

We were not the only ones at a sorrowful occasion; there was a line of blanket-covered bodies.

The first words were those quietly chanted by the padre; "For as much as it hath pleased Almighty God of his great mercy to take unto Himself the soul of our dear brother here departed we therefore commit his body to the ground; earth to earth; ashes to ashes; dust to dust; in sure and certain hope of the resurrection to eternal life through our Lord and Saviour Jesus Christ; who shall fashion anew . . . "

The words trailed away into a mist of memories. As the blanket-shrouded figure was lowered into the ground a tight feeling assailed my throat and I shed a silent tear.

"So long, Fred lad. I'll not forget you. *Arrivederci,* old pal."

The padre moved on down the line of blanket-covered bodies. As a harsh epilogue, Anzio Annie lashed over a round.

Luckily it landed about 150 yards away, on the bottom edge of the burial ground.

The furious cacophony of our gun and mortar fire that day drew the picture of the serious position we were all in on February 18th.

In four weeks an aggressive landing behind the enemy, with the purpose of destroying them, had gone sour. And now we were in a desperate defensive action to prevent us being thrown back into the sea.

In two weeks we had survived two major attacks and now we were in the middle of the third one. One which appeared to be the final one. In the late afternoon of the 18th it seemed doubtful if our last line of defence, the most vital one in the Beachhead - the Flyover on the Albano-Anzio road; the straight road to the port would hold.

If the Germans broke through this we were finished.

Enemy attacks supporting every infantry came forward and as soon as one attack faltered another one followed up, all concentrating on the Albano road, between Carroceto and the Flyover.

News came through at dusk that the 1st Loyals just in front of the Flyover, were being attacked in great strength by German infantry, supported by tanks. The situation was grim indeed but as the time slipped by, on leaden feet, we gained heart; and hoped and hoped and hoped.

One or two snippets of information kept up our spirits. For the first time we heard that thirty German prisoners had been taken. Then the figure rose to one hundred and fifty.

Could it be the first crack? We hoped so.

Bill Queree's death from shrapnel wounds, in number three gunpit of Edward Troop on 19th February desolated me. Coming so quickly after Fred Hirst's death the previous day it was devastating.

With each severing of a link in the chain of comradeship, a chain forged by a sharing of hardships, there were many memories but at the forefront of one's mind there is always one special memory, which one recalls more readily on occasions like this.

About Bill I always remembered the Battery cross-country run at Fyvie, just before we got our KD shorts.

Carrots, in the shape of National Savings Certificates for the winners and runners-up, were dangled before our noses. No exclusion clause existed; except on medical evidence. It was a waste of time to try anything on as a record of the Medical Officer's daily surgery was on file at the Battery Office.

Three of the four in the George Freddy team were not exactly in the first flush of youth. We could truthfully be described as old hacks, with the respective ages of 35, 32 and 30. Unfortunately for the veterans, the leader, the Gun Position Officer (Acting), had the favourable racing age of 22.

Infinitely worse for us was the rumour that he had won something at Officer Cadet Training Unit and while the favourite whisper was P.T. we fervently hoped that the situation had been misread and that his accomplishment had been gained in military studies or some other sedentary course.

Being a very recent addition to the regiment the bushwire whisper had not had the time to be strengthened (or weakened) by hard fact.

In the first mile we found out that athletics had indeed been his forte at OCTU but, strange as it may seem, enthusiasm sometimes does run feverishly in the pursuit of unpopular projects. So we showed our earnest intent to hang on to the bosses heels. Which we barely saw as he gobbled up the mileage.

At the end of the first three miles, and sensing that the quality of our enthusiasm for this particular cause was waning, as shown by our agonised expressions, he slowed up and said to Bill, "Come on, Bombardier. If we don't speed it up a bit George Freddy will be left behind when we get to the run-in at Fyvie Castle. Keep going. Good show."

Bill's bald pate, glistening in the early July sunshine, came a little nearer to us as he made a slow tactical retreat; we guessed he had something to impart.

Bombardier Queree was only thirty years of age but he was as bald as a coot. If you know what I mean. He never got value when he paid for a haircut. Rivulets of grimy sweat trickled through his furrowed forehead, followed the line of his nose and dropped off his chin. His tongue, licking up the ground dust of the foothills of Fyvie, had temporarily losts its power but, within earshot he recovered enough breath to pass on the ginger message to the ancients and threw in, as a bonus, what he thought of the GPO (Acting) at this moment of time.

"Damn it" puff, puff "this is beyond a joke," puff, puff. "Lunatics, at our age" puff, puff, "racing round Scotland for one measly National Savings Certificate, each" puff puff.

"Better move up a bit Bill," said Charlie, "the boss is missing you."

We lost the gist of his last natter as, acting on our advice, he thought the time had arrived for his tactical advance, to renew acquaintanceship with his 'leaders' heels.

Sticking it out manfully, we turned in through the gates at Fyvie Castle having aged ten years in one hour and half.

We were a proud bunch of rookies as we lined up for that fifteen bob Savings Certificate, achieved through being an honourable second. We ignored the ribald comments, which went something like this.

"You're a barmy lot running your guts out for a Savings Certificate. Perhaps as well though, it will help the war effort. You might be in uniform but its debatable if that fact will further it any.

Another sample went something like this

"Hundreds of yards at the double for a penny? Not for me, thanks. You want your heads examining." He was right, we did. Ah, well. There's always two schools of thought; at least.

In spite of it all, at the end of the day, we lined up in pride; none more so than Bill Queree. In spite of his 'puff, puff' - natter, natter and gasps on the taxing route through the valley of the river Ythan, rambling through the foothills of Aberdeenshire.

The mixed experiences shared, the good and the bad, since the establishment of the original George Freddy on 4th July, 1942 were still too fresh in memory to sever any personal links, although he has just earned a lateral transfer to Lance Sergeant in Edward Troop, the sister troop in our own 456 Battery.

*Wadi warfare*

Bombardier (as I would always think of him) Nice Guy, the bank clerk from Jersey, was deeply missed.

But life went on and in the Gun Position command post, below ground the constant flow of messages gave me the thought that at this particular moment of time - the late evening of February 19th 1944 -history was being made and fashioned by the guts of the infantry, up front.

Only one thing was in our favour; the Germans had to advance over open country.

Jerry was determined to push down the Albano-Anzio road and then overrun the Flyover. After which it would be a straight run of ten miles to the town and port of Anzio.

There was not much doubt that February 19th was to be make or break day for us and it looked as if the fate of the beachhead would be decided by the courage of our infantry on the righthand sector, in front of the Flyover bridge.

And so it proved to be.

The Germans succeeded in making a local breakthrough into the Loyals position and one platoon was taken prisoner. Another Company withstood the pressure, with hand to hand fighting, but what had been a second line under stress became the most vital point in a vital sector as the full weight of the German attack was directed against it.

The range of the guns dropped in stages, as the Germans advanced and then - suddenly - there was a glimmer of hope. Their attack eased off and at the same time unconfirmed reports came through that two hundred German prisoners had been taken by the North Staffs on the western sector and two hundred by the Americans on the sector to the east of the Flyover.

The tenacity and bravery of the 1st Loyals, aided by the accurate gunfire of all the artillery on the beachhead had held the massive attack.

At approximately 22.00 hours I reckoned that the 1st Loyals and other infantry regiments had stopped the tide and written the final chapter of this particular bit of Anzioan history.

We took our well-earned rest, content that all the signs and portents - the easing of the German attack, the taking of prisoners along the front and a report from our 309 Battery that the enemy appeared to be withdrawing - were in our favour. We hoped that we had held the biggest attack the Germans had made in the Beachhead since we landed on February 3rd.

In my mind's eye I put the gym shoes back to their rightful spot in my kitbag.- half way down - optimistic enough to think that I wouldn't have to re-enact the operation just yet.

While many more uncomfortable moments were to come and more lives lost, I think it can be said that, never again, was there any danger of us being pushed back into the sea. I hoped that Kesselring had the same thought as I had.

We heaved sighs of relief but recognising that beachhead life was a graph of quick changing troughs and peaks - with a prepondrance of troughs - and that Jerry would have another go very soon, it was a subdued recognition that another trough in our lives would be on the way.

We didn't need telling that we were still on a beleagured beachhead, that the regiment hadn't advanced by a single metre, that Jerry was only three miles down the road and that the initial advance of our infantry had been pushed back and the salient they had created had been nipped out.

One good thing about the situation - and you could count good things on half the fingers on your left hand - was that we could reasonably expect about forty eight hours before the next German attack, and forty eight hours multiplied into minutes seemed a lot of time to help boost morale.

Charlie and I had many profound exchanges on various subjects and if the Generals and Colonels had listened in they would have learned something they could have used beneficially, to the conduct of the war.

However, as the only two phrases they would accept - if they ever got so low in the Military social scale as Gunner/Signaller - were "Yes, Sir" or "No, Sir" they missed a good opportunity.

"Carlo, come peace, I shall remember our chats usually perched on the edge of a foxhole, to reform the world. Tell me, though, why are we stuck at Campo Circus seventeen days after our landing and nearly a month after the invasion? I thought that landings from the sea were planned for the purpose of speeding things up, by getting behind the enemy lines so that the pressure on our friends on the right flank is eased. Personally, I think Jerry's got his second wind and we're stuck. Consolidated too much, I reckon. Rome's still thirty five miles away: same distance as when we landed."

Carlo hesitated, in character, and then countered with sarcasm, the lowest form of wit.

"As well as being a War Diarist you have pretentions to be an Armchair General, have you? An ordinary guy who collects his haversack like everybody else, and then finds a Field Marshal's baton in it. As we're both Sassenachs in a Scottish mob, with no liking for kilts, haggis and the bagpipes - although we have to hide it - will you settle for a bit of profound Scottish literature. Just a thought:- Rabbie Burns said "the best laid schemes of mice and men gang aft 'agley. " That's what's happened, something's "gang aft 'agley. " You're right we've been stuck here too long. Before I go on Command Post duty let me remind you of another piece of Lit. - an Army universal - which says, "Your's not to reason why, your's but to do and ... etc. etc. Cheerio."

"Before you go twiddling the dials and dealing with the phone," I said, "thanks for enlarging my knowledge of Scottish Lit. Whereas before I only knew one quotation from Rabbie Burns, now I know two bits of Rabbie Burns. And they are both very profound. My first acquaintanceship with his wisdom was an entry in my autograph book when I was forced to leave Secondary School and take a job; due to economic circumstances in 1926. My father was a miner. "

"Anyway the quotation was put in by one of my form-mates, a girl, and it said: "Man's inhumanity to man makes countless thousands mourn." And right now don't we know that: we're right in the middle of it. Makes you think."

Charlie giving his usual wry grin, wandered away to his dugout in the Padiglione Woods: the gateway leading to the miserable desolation of an existence lived in a muddy, stinking, wet-earth, close-ended tunnel.

I positively enjoyed the feeling of being on the ration strength of the 2nd Sherwood Foresters, albeit unofficially.

So, on a full stomach of Compo pudding, life at that moment of time was a little different and a little brighter by the shared experience of chats about Derbyshire, about Derby County Football Club, plus some local gossip. Even though I knew that my ears on the return journey would have to be pinned back to listen for 'incomings'.

My luck was in again. I was offered a lift in the Company ration truck, setting out for the wadis and ditches around Carroceto where their forward companies were dug in. On the way there was a convenient junction point to the undergrowth.

The shaky ride on the tailboard of the open utility truck started me on the return journey to Campo Circus and Freddy Troop gun position. Where a night session at the controls of the Command Post wireless set had been detailed on the roster list.

It was a temporarily quiet hour on a late February evening; with a quietness that, in these parts passed all understanding. Over the coastal sector the setting sun filtered its many hued rays over the brooding Campagna. The golden clouds nudged the shaded mauves and an infusion of many hued reds completed a serene picture; if you were prepared to stay awhile and study the sky for a moment, and ignore the rumblings from the north.

So we pulled out of the battalion area. Two men; one infantryman and one artilleryman. Each grateful for the company of the other as we progressed through the void of civilisation. Both of us talkative and both endeavouring to shut out thoughts of the yonder, in front of the Flyover bridge.

Two men; each with a different rendezvous. But I knew in my heart of hearts that mine was the easier prospect. In that selfish way that humans have I was thankful.

Jolting slowly over the narrow bumpy cart-track the slicing of my ear was an imminent possibility as I ducked under the overhanging, wayward branches by the side of the track or when we hit a pothole. My steel helmet had an eighth of an inch over-estimation round the sweatband, giving it a ready tilt.

Our conversation revealed a remarkable coincidence. It transpired that his wife, before their marriage, had lived in my own home village. I knew his father-in-law well.

Small world indeed.

Tongues wagged faster after this snippet of information but before long I had to jump from the tailboard as we approached the junction cart-track to Campo Circus.

"See you in Pilsley, after this lot,-*buono viaggio* and good luck," I said. I held up my hand in acknowledgement as I skirted a bomb crater.

I never saw him again. As is the way of things; both in wartime and in peacetime.

February 22nd was an eventful day, for the Commander of the VI Corps and for myself. For vastly different reasons.

He got the sack and I survived.

Although we seemed to be in a quiet period, between the end of the big German attack petering out on the 20th and the anticipation of another attack in a few days, each day was guaranteed to bring some upheaval. February 22nd was no exception.

To the lower ranks, of which I was a member - a status from which I had never wished to climb from - the 'bushwire' never did fill in the fine detail of its rumours. Strangely, nevertheless, the premature 'gen' had been right in major fact. So we were not disappointed. I didn't admit to possessing any supernatural gift; just an innate gift of adding two and two together and making four.

The sacking of the American Commander of VI Corps, Major General Lucas, was hardly a surprise to me; remembering my comments at the inquest at George Freddy on February 20th on our lack of progress towards the Alban Hills.

I hoped his successor would soon get us out of the mess we were in.

Seeing that in one month we had actually lost ground to the Germans, not gained it, and only barely survived being pushed back into the sea was hardly a recommendation for any top brass to keep his job.

I can't remember the subject matter the same day, when Johnny Fulton and I were having a natter; probably about Number 19 wireless sets, lack of letters from home, or some other general topic.

As the unmistakeable pop of a German 88mm gun disturbed the air we tensed up and dived into the dug-out. Somehow, a sixth sense acquired by experience - told us when one was going to land near, and we guessed that this time it was one that might have our names on.

"Down, Johnny down," I yelled giving him a shove underground, look out, here it comes. "

We lay flat on the floor of the dug-out, chewing the Campagna and waited. There was a loud thud at the back of the dug-out, protected by the roots of a big tree. No explosion, just a thud.

"Hang on a minute," I said, still with the shakes, "you never know. "

After a minute or so we stirred. "Funny thing that, Better wait a bit before we go out and explore. "

Minutes later, things had quietened down and the possibility of another shell to follow it having receded we poked our heads round, clambered out of the dug-out and found the shell, a dud, lodged at the base of the tree.

Rumours had been going round that Czech saboteurs were active and that a few enemy shells had failed to explode.

"I would like to know the name and address of the kind person who filled this one," I thought, slowly ushering myself back to the real world.

The following day a Divisional order was issued emphasising the urgency of reinforcement of weapon pits and dug-outs. Bearing in mind the dud shell incident the previous day I put my shovel into top gear, filled sandbags with Anzioan soil and piled another layer on top.

I recognised that the Divisional Commander of the 1st British Infantry Division knew more than I did about the overall situation on February 23rd. I reckoned that High Command reckoned that it wouldn't be long before Jerry had another go. He still wanted us swimming in the sea.

It was just as if Kesselring had read a copy of General Penney's Order. He opened up with his artillery and the Flyover area of the Albano road copped it. The whole enclave was well within range. The searching shells, apart from the stonk on the main target area, hit the Padiglione Woods and the socalled Rest Areas, two miles nearer the town and port of Anzio.

With the fatalism we had acquired we faced the day-to-day hazards Jerry threw at us; and plodded on.

At half past nine on the morning of March 2nd the rhythmic hum of the Flying Fortresses and the Liberators, with fighter escort, winging their way overhead cheered us up and made sweet music in our ears. About three hundred bombers, with their silvery bellies glistening in the clear air, gave us a strong hint that this could be the beginning of something to set us on our way again. I hoped that the bombing crews, in their cockpits, were sparing a thought for me, below, in my foxhole. Which, after five weeks, I was beginning to hate. Little did I realise then that I had to endure the miserable little hovel for another nine weeks.

To the north the sky was filled with black mushrooms as the German Anti-Aircraft guns searched for the range. Lazily disintegrating, they marked the slate blue sky with a smearing coat of dirty grey.

Suddenly one of the bombers slowly tipped its nose downwards and began a slow spiral, nose-dive to the ground. A few seconds later four parachutes slid from the stricken plane, a black spot dangling at the end of each.

Mentally wetting the tip of my thumb and facing the damp thumb to the north I hoped that there would be a wind reaction slight as it was, I knew that in this confined beachhead, there was probably only one thing; capture. There was no question of landing in No-Man's Land; there wasn't one, to speak of.

The parachutes dropped out of my sight and I knew the query would never be answered for me.

March 3rd was - weatherwise - a deceiving yardstick for optimistic thoughts. The Troop Diary early-morning entry read, "Fair, and improving" and the line of entry stood out favourably against the background of the miserable weather we had endured beforehand.

Grasping at any straw of cheerfulness we were encouraged. But not for long.

The weather turned sour again in the afternoon with frequent rain squalls. Our spirits were dashed by news that Colonel Benson and six other ranks had been wounded. Then we heard that the

Flyover O.P. had been shelled by a German tank; probably the parting gesture at the tag-end of a German counter-attack.

The tenure of each optimistic expectation seemed fated to be short-lived. But then, this was Anzio.

On March 4th both the Medical Officer and the Padre went into dock; unbelievable that it should happen the same day. Bearing in mind their professions, so closely interlinked.

By the second week in March it seemed that pressure from the Germans was easing off. So putting all the straws in the wind together; not forgetting the mixed bag of Standing Orders and the coming of spring sunshine - spasmodic as it was - we could be forgiven for thinking; maybe, maybe.

Maybe we had survived our greatest ordeals on the beachhead and maybe, just maybe, the best was yet to come.

I think it was Samuel Johnson who said "A man who has not been in Italy is always conscious of an inferiority."

This consciousness would never impress a member of either the Fifth or the Eighth Army. Many times in the past year I personally, would have traded in that superiority.

Perhaps when it is all over I shall reconsider and say "I wouldn't have missed it for all the tea in China."

Maybe.

On March 7th we got a new Commanding Officer to replace Lieut. Colonel Benson who had been wounded.

On his second day, almost before he had unrolled his bedroll, the new broom started sweeping. With an avalanche of paperwork, through Regimental Orders. They were marvellous in their variety. They could have been culled from the Notice Board at Woolwich Depot, for the attention of a bunch of rookies sampling Army life for the first time; not for the attention of veterans of the 8th Army on a beleaguered beachhead.

Some Orders were re-runs, others taxed our credulity, while the rest, in the circumstances we were in, were unbelievable in their timing and in their content.

For instance, March 8th "Complete protection against lice and fleas is afforded by AL63, if used in the correct manner." I toyed with the interpretation of the last four words, the phraseology opened up a posibility of putting it in your tea etc. etc. It would have been no good approaching "Snitchy" the Battery Quartermaster, for AL63-apart from not knowing what it was - his raucous voice would utter one sentence, in Gorbals Scottish; "Bugger off, don't waste my time."

Indicating a lack of co-ordination between the CO's words and the Quartermaster's action.

"Units will take steps to preserve and collect as many of their empty beer bottles as possible and will ensure that all available are returned to E . F. I. each week!!!

The exclamation marks are mine.

"Blankets will only be hung out to dry on dull cloudy days"

The CO's inexperience at the wash-tub showed; he should have know that 'shorts, cellular, soldiers for use of' wouldn't dry on dull cloudy days. What chance had horse-hair blankets.

Regimental Order Serial No. 10 12thMarch1944.

1.  Discipline
    (a) Failure to salute.
    (b) Untidiness. Clothes unbuttoned, unneccessarily dirty men, unshaven.
    (c) Smoking while Driving.
    (d) Not wearing arms and equipment on duty.
    (e) Bad maintenance of arms equipment and stores in general.
    (f) Dirty Lines: Kitchens, Latrines

"All ranks will pay particular attention to these points, the observance of which reflects the state of morale and efficiency of the Regiment. The worse the condition the greater will be the effort required."

I was reminded of the one that was posted in Southern Italy, which debarred us from ice cream. "*Niente gelati in Italia*" in a country which invented it and had more ice cream millionaires than anybody.

And so the literary output quickened, and thick and fast came the words churned out by the Regimental clerks in their hole near Stragglers Post; eleven Regimental Orders in twenty three days. Their words of wisdom, intermixed with warning hints were passed like hot potatoes down to the Batteries.

I heeded the implicit warning in Item (b) of Serial No. 10 of March 12th under the general heading of 'untidiness' and decided to get a barber, for a haircut.

It was a calculated risk, in this place, to get a haircut bearing in mind the inexperience of the barbers, the use of blunted scissors which appeared to have in the not far distant past - pruned grape vines, and the knowledge that Jerry, from his vantage point in the Alban Hills, could cover every inch of the beachhead.

Although there was absolutely no possibility of a parade at Padiglione, past experience of being accosted by a tap on the shoulder accompanied by the harshly barked order "Haircut", overlaid with a beery breath laying siege to my neckhole, had laid its hand on my mind.

My selection of barber was rather limited but I thought that Sergeant Bristow of Number 3 gun had shaped rather well in the past. So I got permission to sit on an upended charge case in his gun pit, for the operation.

I perched on the chair and resigned myself to the outcome.

After a score or so snips from the secateurs, from the north came the "pop" of an 88 millimetre. Knowing from experience the limited time margin between "pop" and arrival, we hit the ground and waited with bated breath.

It passed over. I guessed that my haircut would show as many steps as the approach to Caltagirone Cathedral in Sicily; which had quite a few.

I hadn't been aware, when I arranged the haircut, that a spot of recuperation was imminent - two spots in fact. A couple of days later we were detailed for a shower bath (long overdue) and a film show (also long overdue) at a location near San Anastasia, between the Albano road and the coastal sector.

I looked forward to a visit to the Anzio Ritz.

The hole in the ground, for the well-sandbagged cinema, had doubtless been bulldozed by the Americans. They had a much more enlightened attitude for shifting soil from one spot to another than the British had; they preferred bulldozers to shovels.

The film selected by someone with a sardonic sense of humour was titled "Mr. Lucky" and Cary Grant was the star. My assessment was that it was good - no more, no less - but being in a

78

humdrum mood I was capable of exalting an ordinary film to three-star quality.

It did me good and that was all that mattered.

In the early days of March a softness permeated the atmosphere as the warming sun proclaimed a message of hopefulness and the first tentative shoots of the wild flowers and the buds on the trees lifted the spirits.

As I saw the first flowers of spring pushing a way through the green herbage, a sheen of colour that increased in beauty day by day under the daily beneficence of the sun there was a bewilderment in my mind.

Sunshine and blossoming flowers proclaimed a message of life; the constant threat was death. Budding trees and bushes hinted at a beauty to come; the shell-holes and the charred branches, abounding, cast a shadow of foreboding and frustration.

The thought of death here seemed a normal enough thought when the days were dark, rainswept, cold and slimy and when Jerry was putting the presure on. But who wanted to die in a land of spring sunshine, with all the evidence of life coming into the natural scheme of things.

We had faced the possibility of death in sunny climes before; in the Western Desert, Tunisia and Sicily but this lot was the culmination of too long - far too long - in places like this.

I looked down at the brown earth and asked myself, "Aren't these celandines?"

They weren't celandines but the similarity was marvellous and the conjecture had taken my mind back to the marshy edges of the English streams, where they thrived.

After a few minutes in my little world I retraced my steps back to the gun position and becoming engrossed in the daily round and common task the forebodings were blotted out; for a while.

On 9th March hearts were heavy when news came through that Major Colin Patullo, who had been seriously wounded in the previous heavy shelling on the Regimental Command Post had died.

The memory of our old boss, Battery Commander of 456, had not been erased by his recent promotion to Second in Command of the regiment.

Pluto, as we had abbreviated him, was an austere and aloof figure and lacked easy informality. He was never found guilty of breaking into a loud guffaw but there were occasions when a good-humoured glint would appear behind his spectacles, albeit only noticed by the keenest of observers.

His mind was always concerned with efficiency and that, in a war, was good. Our old boss, behind the forbidding exterior had a goodly chunk of humanity which was available in deserving cases. This was my personal considered opinion after more than two years in the Battery.

On the morning of 2nd July 1942 however, I did not consider that humanity loomed very large in his make-up.

With two others, from different parts of the country, we had arrived at Aberdeen station - after embarkation leave - to find that the last local train to Fyvie, fifteen miles away, had gone.

So at short notice, we had to find a doss-house handy to the station, to get a flying start the next morning. We spent that night in a charity hotel in the unsavoury company of dropouts.

Catching the first train the following morning we alighted on the platform at Fyvie approximately an hour after leaving Aberdeen.

Arriving at the Guard Room we heard news which was hardly unexpected. All the way from Aberdeen all three of us had realised that a charge of AWOL was a probability.

From the outset I reckoned we would be on a hiding to nothing. It was known that, in Civvy Street, the boss was in the legal profession so we knew that the hard facts had to be marshalled in good legal order for any of it to be noted in our favour. We knew it would be a futile exercise to try and pull the wool over his eyes.

Confirming our expectations, the message from the orderly Sergeant was; "You three report to the Battery Office, the B.C. wants to see you lot."

His keen eyes bored through us.

"Your order was to report in by 23.59 hrs. on 1st July. You've just arrived; at 09.15 hrs. on 2nd July. What's your explanation?"

"Sorry, sir. The last local train from Aberdeen to Fyvie leaves five minutes before the arrival at Aberdeen of the train from Edinburgh. From the Midlands we have to change at Edinburgh.

80

We had to stay overnight at the Salvation Army hostel at Aberdeen. Here's the chitty. "

Gaining strength from the force of my defence, a big inward monologue was gaining momentum as I thought of the injustice of the charge. "Hey, boss, send your Battery Office clerks on a Railway Time Table Reading Course. Reason, as just outlined to you. They ought to know that from Derbyshire to Fyvie, Aberdeenshire is some railway trip in one day. Then there's the extra hazard of being at the mercy of funny train drivers whose speciality does not include punctuality. Not that the Battery Office clerk will know that Derbyshire is in the Midlands; too far from the haggis, the heather and the bagpipes for him.

That seemed some inward speech but it actually raced through my mind in seconds so the danger of being on another charge, "Conduct prejudicial etc. " was minimal.

"No, sir. It won't happen again. Thank you, sir."

After it had been made exceedingly clear what would happen if other AWOL breaches happened, I was given the benefit of the doubt, marched away, and resumed where I left off at Dunblane.

I daren't mention that on my embarkation leave, unbeknown to me, my mother-in-law had scooped up my battledress and put it through the washtub.

No more would the tall spindly figure of Pluto be striding purposefully through the gun position area ensuring, with legal precision, that everything was shipshape and methodical.

March 9th was a very sad day.

There were occasions when our resolve was under stress and the death of Sergeant Bill Fairburn and the tragic deaths of BSM Alexander and'Dodger'Green of Edward Troop when a German shell hit the cook house of Edward Troop cast a dark shadow over the regiment. The only part of 'Dodger'that was found was an arm.

Our emotions worked on the swings and roundabouts system. which brought an amalgam of humour and tragedy, or tragedy and humour - depending on the sequence or incident and by such a mixture life went on as well as could be expected.

The day Bill Fairburn, a young Scots gun Sergeant, was killed was an illustration of this fatalistic mixture. That day I had acquired, by some influence with the Sherwood Foresters, a pair of trousers, Canadian issue. Walking back from Bedford Street, their rest area, I was feeling chuffed with myself, looking forward to wearing trousers made with smooth cloth. Which would eliminate the itch round the groin which the gravelly British cloth set up.

Having an enquiring mind I had often wondered why the Canadians had smooth material juxtaposed to their thighs while the Britisher had to endure sugar bag hessian and why the Americans bulldozed their Command Posts out and we had to shovel-dig ours.

These questions had exercised my mind since the time we had linked up with the Americans at Kairouan in Tunisia on April 23rd 1943 and supported the 1st Canadian Div. in the Campobasso area on October 23rd.

A long time to wait for the trousers. I knew I would be wasting my time mentioning the bulldozer.

On March 12th, although we had not moved one inch northwards, the combination of the easing of the German attacks, the green sheen of nature from the warming atmosphere and the avalanche of Regimental Orders - signed by the new broom - insinuated, to me, that things were looking up.

That must have been the feeling in the regimental high places as well. For the first time at Anzio a gathering, above ground, apart from combat duties - was countenanced. An interdenominational church service was arranged.

So in a small clearing in Padiglione wood, hard by Campo Circus, about a dozen of us gathered together to hear the word of God, through the words of the Padre. Forsaking all other things, for ten minutes, we prepared - with steel helmets to hand to think about our blessings.

With all the sounds of anger around us, we had to gulp before it went down but I think our presence there acknowledged that there was some sort of belief in the thought.

The service was taken from the Scottish Service Book and the Padre, realising the necessity to cut corners and keep wary ears open, commenced with the prayer on page nine.

Let us pray.

"Oh God, the strength of all who put their trust in Thee, be gracious to us thy servants who are exposed to the perils of war.

Enable us to be strong, to acquit ourselves like men, and to commit our soul to Thee, who alone art our Rock and our Salvation.

Endue our leaders with wisdom and skill, our forces with loyalty and valour. Arm us with might to meet every foe and to endure every hardship. Encompass us with the shield of Thy protection. Bring us again to our homes in peace; through Jesus Christ our Lord. Amen.

"We will now sing verses two, three and four of Hymn Number 72, which fits the circumstances in which we find ourselves. I will give a lead."

"Clear before us through the darkness,
Gleams and burns the guiding light,
Brother clasps the hand of brother,
Stepping fearless through the night;
One the light of God's own presence,
O'er his ransomed people shed,
Chasing far the gloom and terror,
Brightening all the path we tread.
One the object of our journey,
One the faith which never tires,
One the earnest looking forward,
One the hope our God inspires.

"And now let us pray for fortitude, as we go back to our fight against the evils of the world."

Just then although the spring evening clouds, with their glints and shades of red and purple in the western sky over the Tyrrhenian sea, installed an overhang of peace it could not quench the nagging thought at the back of my mind: I hope it's not the Flyover for me tonight. "

"Oh Lord the only refuge and strength of all them who put their trust in Thee, we beseech Thee of Thy goodness so to fortify us, that we may live in quietness of spirit and may serve and honour Thee all the days of our life; through Jesus Christ Thy Son."

"May the blessing of God Almighty, Father, Son and Holy Spirit be with you evermore, Amen."

Mentally strengthened; but still fearful of the coming night. I went back to Number Two Dugout Row; the one with the roof of tree trunks, topped with a sandbag or two and a top layer of soil. The one you entered down two steps, through a door open to the elements, to a floor which was but an uneven portion of the province of Lazio. My mind wandered back to the Empress of Japan, our 26,000 ton troopship, troughing her way through the western approaches of the Atlantic to dodge the U-boats.

My thoughts were of Alan Maycock and Ben Angel who, on the lower deck of a ship with a mixed-bag of 4,500 troops went on their knees, every evening and prayed.

Brother, that required courage, I can tell you.

At two o'clock in the morning a Quad (which hauled the 25 pounder guns) which was parked under the trees fifteen yards away was hit.

We kept our heads down while the ammo inside was exploding.

On March 27th five German planes made an attack on the port area and as we were only $2^1/_2$ miles away we seemed to be right underneath the action.

On the step of the dug-out I gawped, mindlessly, as the German bombers manouvered in the clear blue sky, chased by our fighters.

Talking to myself - not an uncommon achievement - I said "Jerry's a bit active today; bet he's got wind of a big convoy in. The harbour seems to be catching it. "

The words were no sooner formed than there was a ping and a small piece of shrapnel skimmed the rim of my steel helmet and embedded itself in the top layer of sandbags.

"A good job that Anzio has taught you that a steel helmet is a useful article for its proper job, Tommy boy. That was close" said another gawper, nearby.

I never again gazed upwards at an aerial dog fight at such a short range.

On March 29th, in the half-light between night and day, we saw patches of white in the scrubby patch between the south side of the Flyover and the edge of the wood, one hundred yards away.

We found that Goebbels, recognising that the "abcess" was proving difficult to exorcise, was resorting to leaflet propaganda.

One leaflet had a leering skull superimposed over a map of the beachhead area. The misshapen eye sockets were shown as Anzio and Nettuno. On the left side of the jawbone Allied ships were shown going to the bottom of the sea. On the right side Allied planes were crashing into the Tyrrhenian Sea.

"Beach Head - Death's Head" howled the leaflet. On the reverse side it shrieked "The Beach Head is going to be the big blow against the Germans." Wasn't that the slogan of three months ago. Today it is still a beachhead and nothing else, but it is now paved with the skulls of thousands of British and American soldiers. "

"The Beach-Head has become a Death's Head! It is welcoming you with a grin and also those who are coming after you across the sea for an appointment with death."

Another obviously had the intention of causing anti-American feeling. A woman in underwear pulled on her stockings while a G. 1. fastened his tie in front of a mirror . . . "What goes on at home whilst you are away? No woman can resist such handsome brutes
. . .

That one failed as a weapon of propaganda too as the woman in underwear had more close attention than the message.

Over the title The Cassino Debacle" another had a skull topped with a British style steel helmet. A shattered building formed the background. On the reverse side the propaganda 'message' said: "Cassino is still in German hands in spite of huge Allied losses. For weeks and weeks the Allies have been throwing all their resources into the battle of Cassino. 300 Allied bombers dropped more than 2500 tons of H.Es. on the small town of Cassino to blast away the German defenders but when the pounding from the air and the nerve-wrecking barrage had ceased the Germans rose from their foxholes and repelled in hand to hand fighting the massed attacks of the 2nd New Zealand and 4th Indian Divisions who were supported by numerous tanks."

Could that be the German soldier who, according to Allied press and radio is war weary?

And now what about the Nettuno front. Is the slaughter to be repeated there?

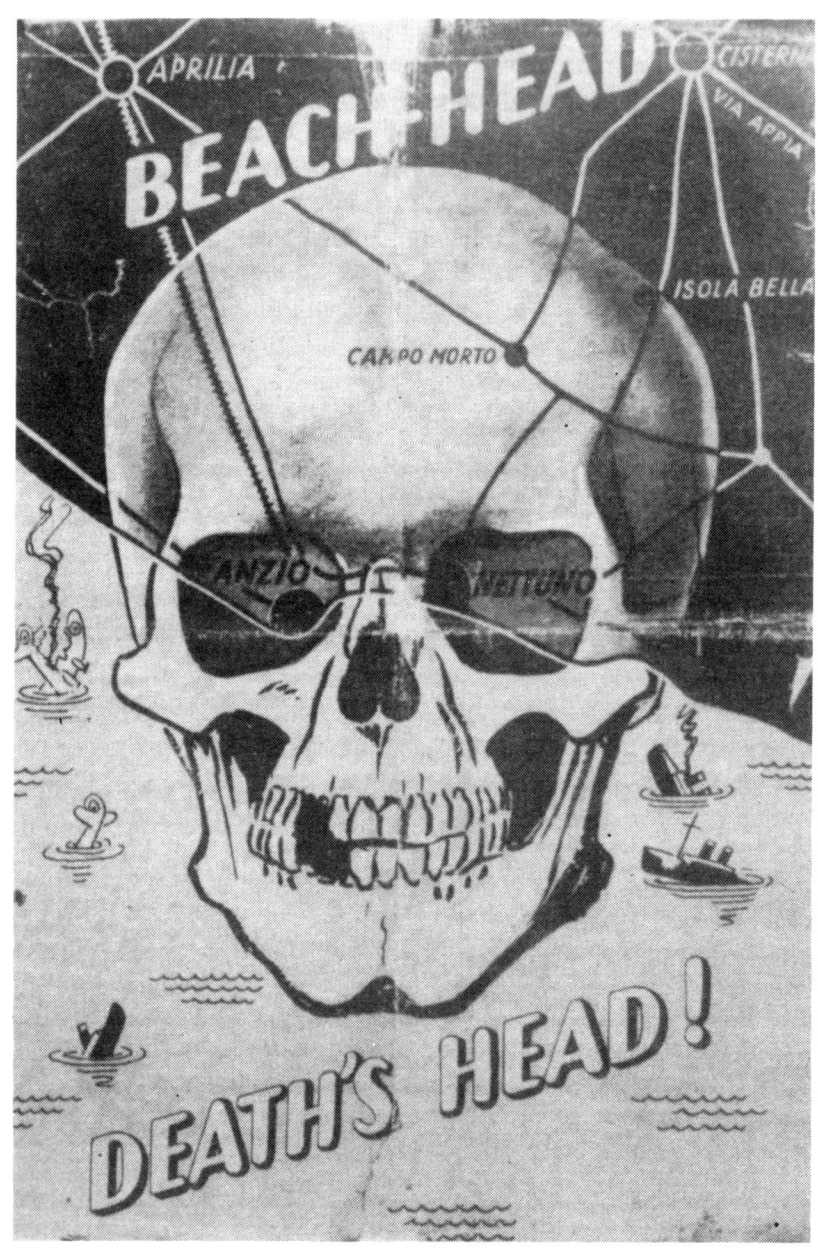

*German propaganda leaflet*

As the leaflets were printed on a smooth-textured paper, silkier by far than the old copies of the Daily Express we had previously pressed into service, we found a purpose for them. On our next short walk with a shovel answering the call of nature.

On April 19th I was detailedfor the Flyover relief party by the Signal's N.C.O. The order "Ready to move at 8 p. m. " reached my unwilling ears and wrought havoc to my peace of mind, in spite of the fact that things were quieter up there since the big German attacks at the beginning of February and then from 16th to 20th February.

Neverthless, I always had an attack of the butterflies on the way to the embankment knowing that the German gunners still had the Via Anziata well registered in their target plans. They certainly knew where the Flyover bridge was.

Only that very day they had registered a direct hit on the aperture to the O.P., which the Sappers had to repair.

As the evening shadows lengthened, with the prologue of a sky shot in irregular patterns of red merging into mauves, we kitted up, loaded up with rations and stores and moved off through Padiglione on our usual route to Stragglers Post, the final left turn on to the Albano road. Where we stopped momentarily to take stock of the situation and take a deep breath.

It proved to be an uneventful journey, which was nice.

The routine tasks of testing the wireless set, setting up the Tommy cooker - with an eye to a brew-up later on - and the various settling-in jobs calmed the butterflies down; despite knowing where you were.

For some reason the night of 19th April was reasonably quiet. As we moved into the dusk of the 20th I was told to get some sleep as the night was likely to be a busy one.

So I coiled up into a human 'S' bend, my knees making a near acquaintanceship with my mouth and my heels arching up to my backside and obeyed orders, as was my custom. I always remembered the castle ramparts. I never could see any material personal benefit in being stupid enough to qualify as a client for the Glasshouse. Especially one overseas.

My eyelids, in the shuttered position -which they had to be to keep out the yellow dust shaken down from the tunnel roof by the landing of German shells on the embankment gave but a shallow impression of sound repose.

A sleep, in the field, was always a light doze and so it was on the evening of 20th April. When fading away from the daily round and the common task into the arms of Morpheus I always sensed what was going on around me. Even when on the doorstep of Phase Two. Perhaps not one hundred per cent aware but so close to it I would have been marked with "Distinction". That's how much I was aware what was going on around me.

So as phrases like "Goliath tank" and "Recovery" fluttered round the tunnel rafters I thought to myself "Ho, ho. Something big on tonight." The word "Goliath", just then, didn't mean a thing to me but later on the jig-saw piece fitted into place.

Goliath was the name that had been given to the German radio-controlled miniature tank which, loaded with explosives, trundled towards its target and then exploded.

REME planned to recover one that had approached the Flyover. Essential information had to be passed on to the 1st Loyals, in their dug-in positions between the Flyover and Carroceto.

The order came through "There will be no tank movements between last light and 0 1. 00 hrs. "

The comings and goings at "Tunnel Villa" made "Exercise Sleep" a non-runner when the clumsy-footed ones, with their size eleven boots, failed to negotiate clearly the space between my knees and my mouth, coiled up as I had to be in the narrow tunnel.

"What the hell," I said to myself "why finish the war with the marks of hob-nailed boots on my face. " So I threw in the towel and made another brew.

At 22.20 hrs. I passed a message back that 'Operation Goliath' was proceeding, followed by another one at thirty minutes past midnight that there was one hundred yards to go.

At one o'clock Goliath was reported through the Flyover bridge and shortly afterwards the success of the recovery mission was transmitted back.

On 26th April vague rumours went around of a possible move out from the beachhead. It was the most wonderful whisper that had wafted our way for ages. Whenever two met behind a tree,

88

each with a shovel and braces undone and with a common purpose, the conversation went something like this.

"Heard we're going off?"

Yes, heard it this morning. Hope it's right. About time."

It was far safer to be behind a tree with a shovel and with braces undone, to fertilise the Campagna at the backend of April than it had been through February and March. Although conversations above ground at Anzio were always fast ones.

The following day rumours of our possible move from the beachhead must have reached the ears of Kesselring's Intelligence Service. The Battery area was plastered by the German artillery. Luckily there were no casualties.

Some *'buono viaggio'!*

In the event our blankets were not bundled up and tied until 5th May. For eleven fraught days, between first rumours and authentic 'Prepare to move', in every man's mind there was an ever-present dread that there could be one with his name and number on it. The last hours of a campaign, of a battle or even of a local move played havoc with ones peace of mind.

At 8 a.m. we handed over to the 67th Field Regt. and at 8.30 the order 'Cease Fire' was given to the Batteries.

We had fired our last round at Anzio.

In preparation for our next move. when Operation Shuttlecock would be inserted into our itinerary - when we would zigzag from the western sector to the easter sector of our Divisional front, finding the highest mountains in the Apennines in the process we buried our surplus bully beef and non-essentials to lighten the load.

If Antonio, or Guiseppe or Giovanni - whichever - when it was all over in his backyard, ever ran his plough on the intersection of Latitude 41.20' and Longitude 12.15', on the coastal sector, he would have struck lucky; on the thesis that "one man's meat is another man's poison." He would have unearthed the delicacy called "bully beef"; the stuff we hated. We were convinced, by the regularity it had been dished out, that the cow population in Argentina had been drastically reduced. We were prepared to bet that the Quartermasters had a vested interest in Fray Bentos.

Antonio, or Guiseppe or Giovanni, if he ever did strike lucky with his plough, would only receive some slight compensation for the upheaval caused to him in having his casa in territory between the Allied and German lines.

The British Army's reward of syringing his houses with D. D. T. seemed poor recompense for having his crops trampled on by milling troops and manoeuvring tanks, and guns, nosing around his best vino, chopping down his fruit trees for fuel and giving him the added worry of keeping his daughters under close surveillance, every time a gun position or a rear echelon invaded his doorstep.

He deserved better than a few squirts of disinfectant from a flit gun.

At 9 o'clock next morning, as the sun was beginning its fast move into the heavens, we moved out from the southern perimeter of Padiglione woods to the direction of the port, approximately a mile away.

We moved out with thankful hearts.

The ordeal was not yet over, however.

It was considered appropriate that our departure merited some 'bull' from the CRA. So at the 'Stand Easy' position in the Piazza, (or what had once been the Piazza, before the surroundings showed their skeletons) cluttered with kitbags, packs and rifle, we prepared, in impatient mood, to listen to the Brigadier's eulogy; with our ears cocked for the popping sound of Anzio Annie, the 280mm. German gun on the railway track. We weren't all that sure that Jerry had quite finished with us yet.

The merit of the eulogy was marred by a restiveness in the ranks; which was a pity because when one has done a job well, it's nice for someone in high-places to tell you so. Especially one with red braid round his service hat.

Soft echoes of the old familiar military anthem "why are we waiting, oh, why are we waiting" rippled below the surface and quietly spoken comments were rife.

"Lining us up here, to hear the same old tripe. Why can't they run us straight on board and away. Too simple, I reckon." or

"A few extra fags or a bottle of beer would be more appreciated just now than all this waffle."

Grouser Tommaso Atkins was at it again, in full spate. Which showed that morale was still at a good level.

The eulogistic phrases fell away; forgotten as the magic word 'dismiss' invaded the heat-warmed atmosphere of the Anzioan morning.

Tension broke and excitement mounted as we gathered our kit together. Loosened tongues gradually eased the tight shackles of a premonition of what might happen.

The sight of L.S.T. 225, moored at the jetty and waiting to take us on board, injected new life behind our kneecaps and at 11 o'clock we embarked on the most wonderful "Skylark" of our lives. After a decade of fourteen weeks we were grateful to be exiting through the door of Hades. Whatever fortune had in store for us in the future, it would be an improvement.

Embarkation was complete at half past eleven and the feel of the gently rocking boat under my feet was terrific. Leaning on the port side rail I saw the quayside devastation fade away in the shimmering heat.

Steaming south we had an air raid warning over the ship's loud speaker. An unidentified plane had been spotted patrolling the coastline on the Gulf of Gaeta.

Nothing happened and we continued on course; to disembark at Pozzuoli on 6th May. En route for Battipaglia, twenty miles south of Salerno, for a re-organisation of the regiment from a 25 pounder outfit to a Medium Regiment.

Battipaglia, an important railway junction on the west coast route to Reggio and Sicily and the cross-country line to Taranto, was a focal point for road and rail communications. It was hardly surprising that its railway marshalling yard had been battered.

The village, resting under the shadow of its Castello, was a haven of rest for numbed minds and weary bodies. All we craved for was a field with some shady trees. Our prayer was answered; we leaguered in an olive grove by the roadside.

Regimental Headquarters pulled rank - as usual - and moved into the castello with its mod-cons; but that only meant four walls and a roof.

The Battipaglian women were kept busy with the laundry. Fourteen weeks of slip-shod washing on the beachhead had to be

91

Battipaglia - Monumento ai Caduti

*Battipaglia monuments ai caduti*

remedied. The little rectangular tins of bully beef found its way into many Italian abodes.

The know-alls said it procured many varied services!

To our delight we found a small stream about one hundred yards down the country lane. Its ice-cold water coming straight down from the torrent-hoarding hills gave relief to jaded bodies. To laze in the refreshing water of the slow-slowing stream, away from the heat of the early summer sun, was a tonic of the finest quality.

What a relief it was not to hear the constant flow of urgent Fire Orders starting with 'Take post, take post' and then the insistent "more -1°, add 200" or "less 2°, add 100 coming down urgently from the O.P. as we covered enemy targets round the Factory, Campoleone, and more worrying still in the dangerous days of the 17th and 18th February, Carroceto.

Just one sentence on the Regimental Orders which read "W.e.f.26/5/44 the 78th Field Regiment becomes the 178 Medium Regiment" caused re-organisation with its consequential upheaval, and crosspostings as we reduced from three Batteries to two. Old standing friendships were disrupted; but the war had to go on.

In effect 456 Battery, being the junior Battery was disbanded and from 26th May, 1944 the two Batteries were 309 and 310.

I ended up in Charlie Troop, Charlie, not Charlies! 310 Battery. Luckily, my signalling pals, Bob Hutton, Charlie Harder and John Hayter remained largely unaffected by the change so that we were able to continue with our normal curriculum, which usually read something likethis.

| | | |
|---|---|---|
| Monday | - | Domestic affairs (English) |
| Tuesday | - | International affairs (what we could glean from out of date newspapers!) |
| Wednesday | - | Domestic (Italian) what we could |
| Thursday | - | interpret |
| Friday | - | Rest Day |
| Saturday and | - | "What's in the Naafi issue this week" |
| Sunday | - | Rest Days (after the fatigues) |

In a word Battipaglia was heaven.

*Charlie troop 310 Battery Palestrina, 15 miles SE of Rome. The author ringed*

The warming sun of the early May days and the simplicity of a life lived in a little bivvy, in a little olive grove alongside a little stream miles behind the action was the kind of heaven we wanted just then.

In spite of the regimental reorganisation, changing our 25 pounders for 5.5 Mediums and the disrupting of the links with some of our mates from the Fyvie days, life gentled on.

It hadn't always been heavenly at Battipaglia. Indeed the village, an important focal point with major road and rail junctions, adjacent to the airfield at Pontecorvino and near the port of Salerno had been attacked and defended on a few occasions.

We stayed training at Battipaglia until July 8th and then with our bigger guns pursued the northward road again.

The Brass Hats, determined to catch up with them again, attached us to 10 Agra at Zagarola.

On 1st August we dropped anchor at Palestrina, the birthplace of the famous Giovanni Palestrina, the 16th century musician.

Such was the peace of the place that we had a Troop photograph taken.

Of the fifty three members, graded from tallest at the back, sitters on chairs in the middle and squatters at the front, approximately fifty per cent had smiles ranging from outright to modest, twenty had a good try but didn't make a show of it, about half a dozen didn't make it either way.

Generously I put it down to a difficulty in interpreting into English the photographer's cliche phrase *parlare formaggio*. Which was, to the uninitiated "Say cheese".

On 9th August we belted along Highway 1 in fast time and for once in a while there happened to be a bit of Italy that favoured us and not the Germans. Also for once in a while we were in the wake of the battle.

At Santa Marinella the gently rolling waves embracing the beach were temptingly visible. We looked longingly and kept rolling along. Feet were on accelerators, not on foot brakes.

We raced along Tyrrhenian coast road, passing Civitavecchia, Chiaroni, Geppetto and Borecchio. The Via Aurelia was uneventful and we took a warning that, look right and you will see, once again the towering Apennines. With the River Arno thrown in as another river obstacle.

Convoy blues existed in the cramped space at the back of George Freddy. The monotonous mileage irked us and Charlie and I began to dislike the sight of each other, cheesed off as we were at breathing down each others neck.

The monotonous march in which there was a rapid succession of mileposts - welcome as they were - irked us. The narrow confined space in the 15 cwt. Humber left for human beings, after the equipment, bedding and wireless set had matured their priority, worked on our nerves.

Thankfully August 9th arrived and at Ginestra in the Pisa area we put the skids on; for a short while. We knew that Jerry had - once again - stopped, fixed his favourite spot for defence, changed from mobile to static; and dug his toes in.

We faced up to the fact that we figured in the plans being made by General Mark Clark and General Alexander to crack the Gothic Line.

Rumour had it that they hadn't been the best of buddies since Anzio. Talking about rumours, I always felt that the best thing to do was to believe the ones that didn't hook you on to a rosy thought of the future and not to get too chuff about future possibilities. That way you didn't drop too hard when adverse reality set in. If the good rumour turned up trumps you had a bonus. It rarely did.

Buddies or not, Alexander and Clark had to get down to position their polyglot divisions into place to tackle the Gothic Line which ran from Pisa in the west to Rimini on the Adriatic, in the east. A front of 150 miles.

So the cosmopolitan divisions of Poles, New Zealanders, Canadians were placed on the eastern sector, the Indians and the British in the middle and the South Africans, Americans and British left of middle. Oh, I forgot the Brazilians, left of centre.

The 6th South African Armoured Division was our next port of call so, as the Armies took shape for the last crack I reckoned it wouldn't be too long before I would be reading an ancient copy of the Cape Argus again, which pleasure I hadn't had since our call in Capetown with the "Empress of Japan" on Friday, August 14th, 1942.

By a series of eastward moves we approached the foothills of the northern Apennines; Better for us to be digging - in on mountainsides than on flat ground, the Brass Hats thought. But to be fair to them there was far more mountain than flat plain in the Gothic Line.

We guessed that we were on the doorstep of the serious business; once again.

# CHAPTER FOUR
### The Gothic Line.

Ginestra brought us back to the edge of battle stations. But first things first. We thought of Santa Marinella and built our own swimming pool; ten yards long and four yards wide.

For a troop of about one hundred men it was hardly ideal but on a rota system it was a temporary haven for dusty bodies.

The Brigadier at 10 Agra hated to think that the 178 Medium was leagured on flat land so ordered us on a regimental sidestep to Campi.

Bovecchio breathed a warning that the highest mountains in the northern Apennines were just round the corner and we edged nearer at Calenzano on September 12th, Barberino on the 19th and Montepiano on the 27th.

The guns were not allowed to get rusty.

At Monzuno'Toc'Kerr and myself were out repairing another break in the line when Jerry lashed over a salvo of three 88mm. shells on to the cart track linking the Command Post and the O.P. We dived for cover in a deserted cottage, leaving the teeing-in phone on the track, aiming to recover it when things had quietened down. In our hurried scramble for cover we reckoned that one Don 5 telephone was cheap enough in a war.

That was our mistake.

The Battery Commander soon removed that impression with a terse order from the Command Post, "Find that phone. " I got the distinct impression that there was a whiplash threat of "or else" tagged on at the end of the instruction; in tone of voice, anyway.

Our thoughts of Battery Commanders in general had never been bathed in a rosy hue. But, then in a military establishment a general principle was that ordinary rankers detested Sergeants, Sergeants detested Warrant Officers, Regimental Sergeant Majors were anathema to Warrant Officers and everybody danced to the officers' tunes.

But then came exceptions to the general rule and humanity reigned. This enabled a squaddy to retain his sanity.

In this particular incident the opinion we had of the Battery Commander who owned us at this particular moment of time was mutinous; but mutiny at long distance. Albeit that for a long time we had realised that signallers were of the lower order of the Army species the news that two signallers did not equate to one common telephone was a sobering thought.

The pedigree of the bloke at the other end took a sharp nosedive towards an unknown parentage; only rescinded an hour later when South Africans of the 6th Armoured Div. mollified us; assisted by retrospective thoughts that perhaps our feelings and remarks had been aroused at a time of stress, and therefore a little warped.

The only clue we could pick up was that two South African signallers had been seen going back up the track to the main street of the village. We thought they might know something.

So, when we considered that Jerry had shed his spite against us and that things were quiet, we ventured out and back-tracked to the village.

We searched out the Command Post. The door would not give, and only after a concerted effort of pushing and shoving did we get in.

Then we saw the reason for our struggle to gain access. Wooden case on wooden case and cardboard carton on cardboard carton took up all the available space, jamming the door.

We gazed in goggle-eyed amazement on a ceiling-high mound of Christmas parcels for the 6th Armoured S.A. Div. Our faces gave our thoughts away.

To the laddy from the sunny climes we explained the situation about our telephone. "We left it on the track; couldn't find it when the shelling was over. A Yank said he thought two South African lads had recovered it."

Pointing to the corner of the room he said, "that's it. Our fellows thought something had happened to the signallers who owned it and brought it in. Like one of those cakes?" he asked.

Toc Kerr beat me to it and in his best Edinburghian accent said "Och, aye *grazzie,* thanks a lot". As cosmopolitan a selection of thankfulness as you could get, but it fitted a memorable occasion for the cosmopolitan gang of South African, Scotsman and Englishman.

That cake baked with sunbaked fruity sultanas from Cape Province, and given spontaneously, went down well.

Perhaps we deserved it, supporting the Witwatersrand Rifles.

At Barberino we dived into the miniature heaps of discarded "K" rations, left behind after a disastrous attempt by the Americans to capture an important high point. In our search for ration change, we foraged unceasingly for the tiny cellophaned packets of Yank biscuits and cigarettes. We burrowed into the mound like a bunch of Itie kids poised round our own swillbins.

Such is the way of things, after a short period on "K" rations and PX stuff British rations regained its lukewarm popularity.

I always reckoned that the stock of tinopeners cooks for the use of, to open the bully beef (in tins) the cheese (in tins) and the jam (in tins) took up a goodly proportion of shipping space, but the loss of a tin opener could have been catastrophic. Although the dog biscuits would still be liberated for issue.

Second thoughts; they would probably be in tins too.

At Monzuno, we shared billets in a hovel with a tank crew of the American 1st Armoured Division. As always, in action and out of action, the generosity and comradeship of the GI's was memorable. Unfortunately, according to the bushwire, that was not always so at Brass Hat level.

Of life in action it could be said that acquaintanceships, of necessity, was of the ships that pass in the night variety. Fleeting and recordable in ones memory, or fleeting and not worth a further thought.

Sergeant Stank and his mates were of the first variety.

On the second morning they told us they were moving out to the western sector.

"We hear the Brazilians are in trouble. Take these rations. You don't get supplied with smelly soap by your Q blokes, do you?" the sergeant chortled, handing over several tablets of perfumed toilet soap and surplus food rations. "Plenty more in our PX. They'll do you boys some good Shucks, that's all right, forget it. Let's know how you fellers get on. O.K.?"

"O. K. We will, *Buono fortuna,* Mind how you go, Eddie."

"All the best, fellars. Let's go."

"Roe," said Sergeant Eddie Stank, of Scranton, Pennsylvania, stopping at the door and looking back, "If you ever come across to the States after the war don't forget to look me up. Here's my home address. There's nothing that would please me more than to see you and swop stories after this lot's over."

"O.K. Eddie," I replied. "If I ever do cross the Atlantic I'll pop in to see you."

Momentarily my grasp of American geography eluded me so I was going to pop in just as if I had only a few streets to negotiate instead of some hundreds of miles. "Nice to have known you. *Arrivederci.* "

We moved on too; to support the 6th South African Armoured Division based in the Lagaro area.

On 28th September, as evening dusk was dropping its shutters across the darkening landscape. George Freddy got a detail to mount an intermediate wireless station at Montepiano, on the Florence-Bologna road. Screening, made by a combination of being a densely wooded area, at a height of 3,200 feet above sea level, made wireless communication between the O.P. and the Battery position very disturbed. Very few clear signals were getting through.

Len Taysum, one of the best drivers in the Battery, was assigned to take us in a half-track to the vicinity of Montepiano.

The undulations of the landscape, which rose sheer on the starboard side, and dropped into deep ravines on the port side, was not helped by the fact that there was a covering of about three inches of snow. On a clear evening, fleecy white clouds were playing hide and seek with the stars, on a background of slate blue. A screen of coloured sameness covered the night. So that there was no clear distinction between the sky and the road.

Monte Coroncina, overlooking Montepiano, thirty miles north of Florence and roughly equidistant between Florence and Bologna, sneered at us from a height of 3,800 feet.

The minor road, our axis of advance, had to be negotiated with caution. The urgency of the situation had to be balanced with the necessity for Len to keep his eyes glued on the road. Being in a

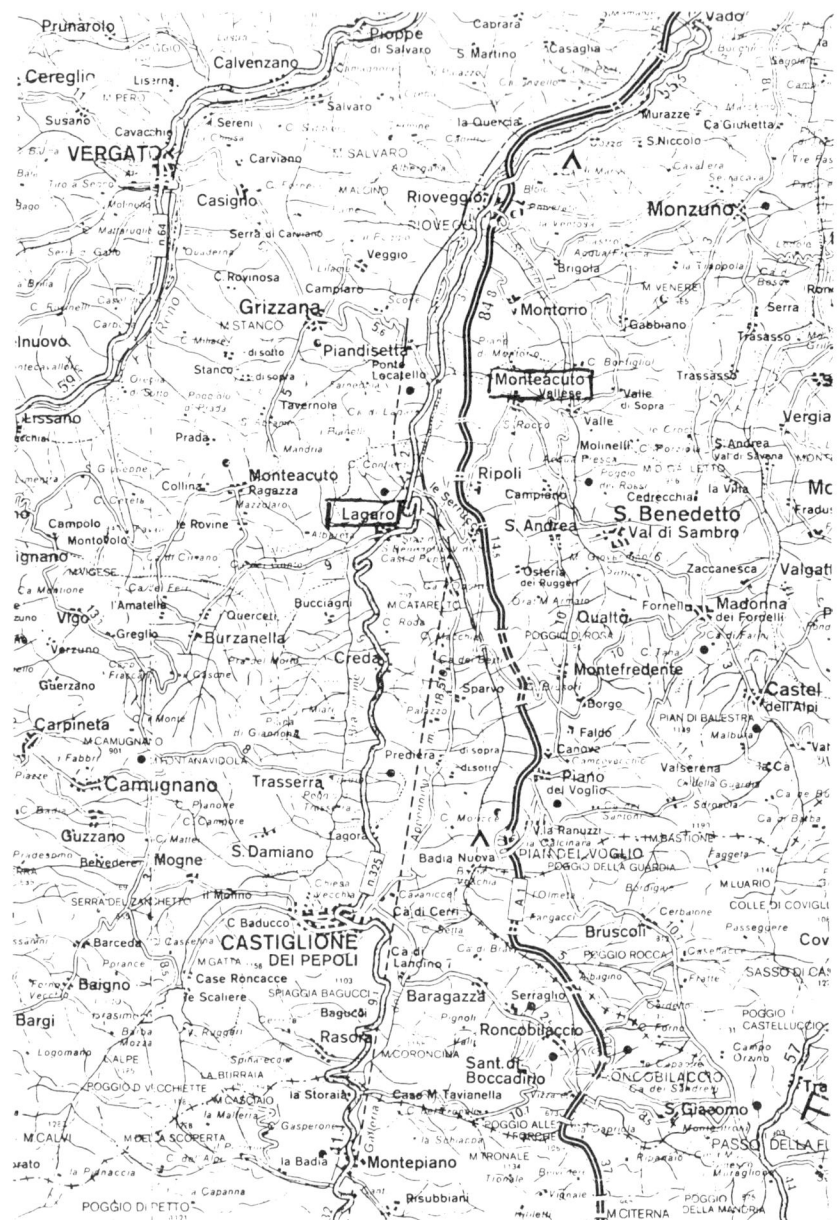

*Lagaro base Monteacuto OP and Vallese.*

102

half-track meant that the field of vision for the signallers was limited to the sides of the vehicle.

All at once pandemonium broke out.

"Stop. Hey, stop, stop," bellowed Charlie Harder, threatening my ear drums. You think this truck will ride on that white cloud you're taking it on to? Do you?"

Len's reactions on the brakes were immediate and we jolted to a halt.

A quick intake of breath and Charlie said, "Sorry, Len, no disrespect. "

The Brummie's comments were consistent with his usual brand of instant wry wit. "Rather have your disrespect, Charlie, and stay right way up on this road than to be down at the bottom of that ravine. Thanks, pal."

The fleecy white of the evening clouds had beckoned us to a right hand turn which brought us to the very edge of a deep ravine.

We backed out carefully and went on our way.

To no avail. We were screened out solid, failed to establish wireless communication and had to return to base.

At the end of a guard duty the sweetest part of any day was the sight of the first timid probings of the dawnlight sky, filtering hesitantly over the mountain tops and in minutes gaining strength. The tensions of the night relaxed as the treetops emphasised themselves against the cleansing skyline.

The clattering of the dishes, pots and pans communicated the message that the cookhouse had heeded my call to "wakey, wakey" given an hour before. I knew that, in accordance with tradition and unwritten law, my reward would be a mugful of hot and sweet tea; and a chance to warm my backside against the cookhouse fire. Temporary morale booster as that was, it nevertheless was a help to face the coming day. Starting the day with a mug of cookhouse brew inside you was a fillip. Everybody knew that cookhouse tea had plenty of body in it; more than the measly allocation of tea, sugar and milk the trucks would be allowed.

Our gallop to the Alps was stopped in the Emilian Village of Lagaro, roughly midway between Florence and Bologna. The snow covered mountains and hills and the overfull rivers and streams in our sector the Setta and the Reno, and its tributary the

Sambro put paid to the hope of a move northwards. Until the winter snows melted from the slopes of Monte Stanco and Monte Salaro there was not much hope of an advance.

Routine changeover of O.P., intermediate and maintenance posts took place regularly and the right hand turn from the main street, which was the only one that Lagaro possessed, down the winding side road that wended its way downhill between the chestnut woods to the ice-cold waters of the fast moving Sambro and then climbed sharply to the railway station and tunnel of San Benedetto became all too familiar with the passing days.

"Does the road wind uphill all the way" had been asked before.

In the Apennines it does. They wind round like corkscrews, were littered with ravines and for good measure, when you get round the corner, another bloody great mountain peak stared you in the face.

So in that holdup from 6th October, 1944 to 14th April, 1945 we got to know Monteacuto Vallese, a haven of peace Well, comparatively, amidst the harsh realities of a winter campaign in a static position. We were still disturbed by the zooms, whirrs and crashes of incomers from Jerry.

Monteacuto Vallese, a peasant hill village where only the bare necessities of life appeared on the agenda of the natives; in the material sense. But for us, on the balance sheet of life, there was the overwhelming credit of a wonderful bonhomie for the interloping *Soldati Inglesi.*

In that typical peasant house perched in the left hand corner of the little quadrangle; quadrangle in villages, piazza in towns and cities with one side open to the winding road to the south and the other three sides concealing us from the prying German eyes in the hills opposite, three miles uphill from Lagaro, Guiseppe became like a brother, Maria of the large bulk and larger heart a considerate *sorella* and Mama, blessed mama, made us feel that we were not interlopers but that she had taken two more sons into her entourage.

Monteacuto Vallese became special, very special to Charlie and me. I knew it would always remain so in our memories to the end of our days; however soon that might be. It became a haven for two ageing signallers of the 8th and the 5th Armies, just a little weary from scufting sand (only to see it fall back from whence it came), from a dissection of the Apennines while slogging upwards from Point So and So to Point So and So, netting to Control, passing Fire Orders, slushing through the ice cold waters of the River Sambro in the valley and climbing chestnut trees a speciality in the area to loop a telephone line on the bankside, to ensure that Nagel spoke to McKenzie and Hunter spoke to Oram.

Around the north east corner of the last house in the quadrangle a long sweep of enemy occupied country dominated our hill top, and also the valleys of the rivers Reno and Setta, with its tributary the Sambro. Beyond the cover of the peasant cottages it was 'full view' country for about two hundred yards, so the pigmy approach, knees full bend and head ducked, was the order of the day, as we sallied forth to reach the sanctuary of the hedgerow on the cart-track to the treeenclosed church.

On 30th September, on detail, we sallied forth and negotiated the danger area safely. The tension eased and the conversation turned to light chatter of the gossipy sort.

White-shrouded infantrymen, crouching in scattered twos and threes under the shelter of the shortboughed defoliated hedgerow, were peering intently through binoculars for sign of enemy movement in the wooded areas of Monte Catarello. They stared in open-mouthed disbelief as Bill Wann, a Scot, and I came down the track, unconcernedly discussing the prospect of Glasgow Rangers in the Scottish Cup and the London and North Eastern Railway, who had us both on their payroll.

"Cor blimey, stone a crow. Keep your bleeding heads down, will you. 'Presto' What mob has the misfortune to own the pair o' you, eh? Artillery? Thought as much. Via' before you draw something down on us."

Temporarily bemused by the fact that the expected Lanarkshire accent of the Scots Guards had changed for one that smacked of the Edgware Road in London, I could only mutter, "In view here, are we?"

Which was a lame enough enquiry, in the circumstances.

Still decoding the unprintable reply after two hundred yards down the narrow track, the tree-enclosed church, our pinpointed right turn, came in  sight. We eased ourselves through the hedge

105

and followed the telephone cable downhill, to the valley of the Sambro, hugging the hedgeside cover as we went.

After half an hour's steady progress downhill we reached the western bank of the river. Fed by numerous small tributaries flowing down from the mountain tops, it was in full spate. The line being checked all clear to that point, we realised that our luck was out and that the break in the line must be on the other side of the river. The prospect of having to wade through the racing frothy water, in vulgar parlance, "knocked our ducks off."

My first tentative steps into the ice cold waters of the Sambro crinkled my hair. As I progressed, the high watermark on my legs gradually crept upwards; first ankle height, then calf depth and then kneecap depth. I said a silent prayer that I hoped that this river was not in the same league as the Sangro and the Garigliano and pressed on.

My prayer was answered; I maintained kneecap level until I reached safety on the other side, about thirty yards downstream from where I started. I appreciated the fact that the German gunners had not zeroed on this bit of valley. Soaked to the skin up to the knees, demoralisation set in. I was as miserable as Hell.

On the rising ground, about a hundred yards to the east, we found the break in the telephone cable, repaired it and teed-in to the Command Post. Communication being established, we could begin to kill Germans again.

We went on our way not actually rejoicing, but in a better frame of mind.

Admitting to myself that my sense of orientation was adrift I looked around in the gathering dusk. The scenery was the usual mixture in the upper Apennines; defoliated trees in a desolate, cold, bleak and wooded countryside, stacked with mountain peaks of three thousand feet high and more.

Suddenly I saw a brownishred roof standing out in a copse of sapling trees. At this height from sea level and in this climate a roof presaged a haven. Or an enemy outpost.

Being south east of me I reckoned, in spite of my orientation problem, that it was on the friendly side, on the basis that any location south, be it south east or south west was on home ground. We decided to reconnoitre the roof.

It was a haven indeed; a forward cookhouse of the Scots Guards.

Rehabilitated with a mug of hot sweet tea and an exchange of pleasantries we were set on course to find our way back. We re-crossed the Sambro and started the uphill climb back to our village.

It was then that I started to come apart. I said to myself "Tommaso, you're buggered. You'll never make it." I felt 135, not 35 years old.

My weary feet were sucked back into the muddy morass as I began the leadenfooted trudge through the ankledeep ooze. Desperation began to set in as I realised that there was about another mile to go three quarters of it uphill through the clogging mud and that with the advent of darkness, my tired legs would never be able to sort out the best bits to land on.

The slow drag of one foot after the other drained me of all feeling. I could have laid down, not caring overmuch if this cruel field was to be my last resting place.

Bill, sizing up the situation, had different ideas.

Thanks to my buddy who cajoled, coaxed and slowly shepherded me the rest of the way, we hit Paradise in the little quadrangle, where mamma, the ministering angel, took over and told the juvenile GPO, way back at Lagaro, that he couldn't have his signaller back; for that night, anyway.

So, for one night, Mama took charge of part of the British Army and the George Freddy signallers were delighted to hear that immature and bumptious Lieutenant, way back at Lagaro, put in his place by a lovely Italian lady. Doing what we would have loved to do; so many times.

Small wonder that we shall always remember Monteacuto Vallese, between the rivers Reno and Setta and 3,500 feet up, between Florence and Bologna.

Winter having imposed a stalemate on large scale operations, it was possible to send leave parties, in rotation, to Florence.

On 29th November my name came out of the hat for the prize of five whole days in Italian Renaissance country.

Window gazing at the finery and the Florentine jewellery delighted our eyes, and paybook credits took a beating.

The film "Fanny by Gaslight" beckoned invitingly from the hoardings of the cinema hired by "Welfare" but Fanny, somehow, had no attraction for me.

I recharged my mental batteries by leaning on the southern riverside wall on the River Arno, comtemplating the beautiful sunset and admiring the grandeur of the Ponte Vecchio; the only bridge in Florence left standing by the Germans before their retreat to the north. The desolation of the rubblestrewn river banks alongside the other two bridges, the San Trinita and the Carraia, which had been destroyed, told a sad story.

The castellated tower of the Palazzo Vecchio, set against the background of a magical sunset, was a memorable spectacle. A sight worthy of being registered in one's book of memories. The peace of the Tuscan evening spread a feeling of serenity and anchored my bewildered thoughts, running round in circles.

A tide of nostalgia swirled my mind over the Apennines, over the Swiss Alps and beyond; to a little Derbyshire village where I knew my dear wife was patiently waiting and where my two daughters aged eleven and two were growing up far too quickly without me.

As we set out for the return journey the cheery spontaneous ribbing of the outward journey was missing and on the journey back to American Fifth Army country at Lagaro the conversation was desultory and well spaced out.

"What's next?" was the thought uppermost in all our minds as we turned the corner at Castiglione dei Pepoli seven miles from our destination.

Snowcovered one-street Lagaro, packed with the vehicles of the 6th South African Division, welcomed us back and we dropped into a layer of snow and into reality.

We picked up where we had left off; covering targets for the Imperial Light Horse and the Kimberley Rifles in the 6th South African Armoured Division.

The winter snows halted my journey back to Derbyshire; I waited for the spring sunshine to soften out the harsh reality of winter, four thousand feet up.

Just before Christmas it snowed and it snowed, until we had a dept of two feet. The Signals truck and other soft vehicles of the

6th South African Armoured Division parked on both sides of the only main road Lagaro possessed, were covered.

So the first hint of what to expect in the coming months, arrived in a white mantle.

Visits to Peacock O.P. became all too familiar and on the side of the winding uphill road we saw a railway engine which had been dumped there by a bombing raid on San Benedetto station yard.

When the last uphill climb became too much for the Jeeps we had to resort to mules, and the mules were no more enthusiastic that I was to clamber up the goat-track to the isolated farmhouse, logged on the Command Post map as Peacock O.P.

I spent my thirty fifth birthday, Boxing Day, pushing on the rump of an awkward mule and then on my belly peering through binoculars for signs of enemy movement on the hillside across the valley.

There was no movement.

At night, under the artificial moonlight, the countryside looked romantic. It was more romantic coming back from Peacock in the mountains, than going out to Peacock, in the mountains. Such was the relief to get an O.P. duty cover.

I remember my first visit to Peacock very well.

We dossed down on the floor of a barn which was covered by a layer of straw, which looked in pristine condition.

Luxury indeed, we thought. "O. K. for a kip here."

After half an hour it was nicely warm under my backside. After an hour it was itchy, hot and unbearable. We found that the bottom layer, on the floor, was a mixture of straw and oxen dung; the end product of the normal four-legged occupants.

There was a treat in store for us when we got back and our spirits rose when we heard that Jennifer Jones, bless her heart, had called in - on celluloid - for our entertainment. "The Song of Bernadette" projected on the back wall of the village hall enthralled us. Just then Micky Mouse would have done the same!

The winter snow, with Monte Stanco and Monte Salaro to the north, towering to a height of 2,500 feet, and the twin fast flowing rivers of the Reno and Setta all in full spate were solid reasons for the holdup. We were enclosed in a triangle of snow, high mountains and turbulent rivers.

Monte Sole, on the left, sheltered the keen searching eyes of the Germans.

So December and 1944 disappeared from the calendar and under the aegis of the greenbordered yellow triangle of the 6th South African Armoured Divison we waited for the sun to shine and the snow to melt.

And Gamecock OP was approached by just as miserable a goattrack route and the misery was accentuated when "The Babe" was OP officer.

Nicknames, I always thought, were latched on people as a mark of some sort of esteem; in this case it was latched on the Lieutenant as a summing up of his antics which, to men nearly twice his age, seemed positively juvenile. Say; an inexperience in the game of life which possession of one pip didn't hide.

Inside Gamecock OP, a peasant's cottage set on the rolling hillside and submerged in the wintry scene, friendliness belied the uncompromising exterior, where there was no sign of the message 'Welcome'on the mat outside. But inside was different;'Welcome' was certainly on the indoor mat as soon as we stepped over the threshold.

Normal life, to the peasants in this chestnut forest area, was very austere indeed. The staple diets were polenta a sticky pinkish mess, chestnuts and spaghetti. The polenta pot, hanging on the tripod over the open fireplace, fuelled by the aromatic firewood, always seemed to be on the stir.

*Martedi, polenta; Mercoledi polenta; Gioverdi, polenta; Venerdi polenta; Sabato polenta; Domenica polenta;* and the one I've missed, *polenta. Sempre polenta.*

It was said that on the clearest of days, the towers and spires of Bologna could be seen if you looked closely enough.

I never saw them; because *bruto tempo* obscured everything.

On one occasion at Gamecock we were saddled with 'The Babe' as 0. P. officer; when he decided to test out his partiality for spaghetti,Tuscany style and put his appetite on public exhibition.

A huge bowlful was placed before him on the roughhewn table and as forkful after forkful disappeared down his gullet the bowl was soon emptied.

We watched in silent, but discreet, amazement when he made a request for more; and did the same to the second helping.

The padrone's wife threw us a pleading look which we broadly interpreted as "please get him a posting" (this word was our interpretation for an Italian word we didn't understand).

Language difficulty or not, I interpreted her pleading glance as we moved out to go back to Lagaro after our three day duty. I'm sure she said "*questa tenente, non pui, non pui, per favore.*

Which meant "please don't bring him again."

I gave her a sympathetic glance but what influence had I to transfer a guzzling officer. Precisely; nil.

In the meantime the evening news sessions, after closedown of the wireless net, became like a meeting of the local Defence Committee where most of everybody had their say. Italian tongues wagged increasingly and undulated like the mountains and the valleys; up and down.

As I said, Charlie with his avuncular style was very popular but one day, good pal that he was, he tipped me the wink that I was catching him up. It appeared that some whispering had been going on that I ought to be canonized as San Tommaso of Monteacuto Vallese (how I would have got that lot on to an envelope I don't know!)

Deflation set in when it leaked out that the award had been sarcastically suggested, when it became known that I was a non-smoking non-drinking freak.

I bore no malice; it showed they were thinking and talking about me; and that was nice to know.

I hoped that the aura of San Tommaso would linger on in the memories of the radio news listeners in that mountain *villagio* in clear weather within spire distance of Bologna and in *bruto tempo* obscured in everything but our dreams when I had moved on.

The early days of January 1945 were heartwarming ones. The Russian offensives were storming towards the German border and the eastern half of Western Poland had been overrun. Only the River Oder lay between our Allies and Berlin. The thoughts of what Marshals Koniev, Rokossovsky and Zhukov were doing on the Oder, the Vistula and in East Prussia cheered us up; and Charlie got bigger audiences for his translation of the war news.

The tremendous implication of the wireless news readily settled into the British soldiers' hearts, occupying Monteacuto Vallese in the cold wintery province of Emilia, in a friendly manner.

With our own hopeful hearts and a captive peasant audience, agog for the news, we first switched to the B.B.C. news after closing down on the Battery net, and then to Radio Roma.

Charlie, having been taken affectionately to the hearts of the Monteacutions by reason of his slight advance of the pidgin variety of the native language, was securely entrenched in the family circle as 'Amico Carlo'.

His patient renderings and interpretations of the radio news bulletins, accomplished by many tolerant sweeps of his blackened pipe towards Mama, Maria and Guiseppe made him a little tin God in their eyes. Personally, although he was my long standing buddy, I thought they took it just a little too far.

On this particular evening, he switched on to Radio Roma and a hush descended on his captive audience. At the end quizzical looks were exchanged between the natives and Charlie took this as his cue. "Dialetto" difficulty as between Roma and Emilia defeated them, so Carlo's pronouncements were awaited with bated breath. With much nodding of aged heads there were repetitions of " *Tedesci finito*" or "*Si, si Tedesci finito, kaput,* " or perhaps more hopefully "*La guerra finito subito, eh.* "

To Mama, the mother and Maria and Guiseppe her family, peasants living the simple life in a mountainous region of the backbone of the Apennines an area of chestnut forest spaghetti, polenta and chestnuts were important ingredients of their staple diet. The sheer monotony of it appalled us and it didn't take us long on our very first visit to Monteacuto Vallese in fact to make an arrangement.

We shared their spaghetti and their chestnuts (but not their polenta) and they shared our M & V; our bully beef and the chocolate and the other few luxuries which invaded Tuscany, via Lagaro and the Naafi truck.

We were all happy at the arrangement; particularly the Britishers who were trying to repay Italian kindness.

On a quiet evening my fatalism inbred quite strongly now decreed that first things came first and indicated that I would relish a dish of roasted chestnuts for the evening meal.

So I reached for the colanderlike bowl with the three foot long handle, hanging on the wall, and Mama filled it with chestnuts. Then I pushed it over the wood fire. The real art, which I never mastered properly, was to shake and turn, turn and shake, the chestnuts to make sure that they were all nicely roasted but none were burnt.

Having gorged myself into a dreamy state on a starchy diet I was in a contemplative mood, fostered by the confident thought that the night of January 9th was going to be a quiet one because Jerry would not have the inclination to bother us that night.

I wouldn't have signed a contract on that thought, but the feeling was firmly lodged in my bones.

And so it proved to be; a night with no broken telephone lines and with a wireless silence.

In the middle of January while increasing my knowledge of the Apennines at a new position, one and a half miles north west of Lagaro, "Wicky" Wickenden and "Slag" Bailey were my mates at an intermediate wireless station in a deserted peasant cottage. The normal residents had temporarily lapsed their tenancy, so we were down to basics.

Not an unknown situation.

At Sousse in Tunisia, Slag and I had shared the first prize in a Morse Code competition, in the Battery for speed on a Don Five phone; which couldn't be pushed for more output. My Civvy Street experience on a London and North Eastern Railway Company's telegraph instrument served me well at Sousse.

My pleasure at being equal top of the tree was diminished when, for my prize, I was handed a small tin of fifty cigarettes; probably the weekly ration of somebody who was in 'dock'.

For a nonsmoker from the age of fourteen when I had tried one or two, got caught in the act by my dad, a compulsive smoker, and got a belting which was sufficiently persuasive to make me a nonsmoker for the rest of my life. Another very important factor in my mind at a more mature time in my life, was that I realised the stupidity of paying out money, to make myself a member of a smokers' club, the main aim of which was to ensure a shorter life.

In the mid 1920's decade of struggle and strife in the mining industry, which was our livelihood, I think my dad thought that two smokers in the same family was one too many and seniority on the family tree indicated that I was the one to go. Plus the fact that I could not, find the wherewithal to finance a twopenny packet of Woodbines.

Twenty one years later my prize, like my weekly free issue, ended up in the bowl of Charlie Harder's ancient saliva-scorched pipe; never far from having an acquaintanceship with his teeth.

The next attack against the Germans was due against Monte Belvedere, towering to a height of 3,400 feet on our left front.

"Hey, Slag" I shouted, "you heard that message from the Troop Commander that the O.P. set has conked and they want a replacement "*subito*". We're detailed to take it. I reckon it will be a goat track do, with wear and tear on the kneecaps, after scrambling through the scrub on tracks where a goat would turn its nose up.

"I don't suppose that either of you two, with your innate sense of chivalry, will volunteer the information given quite freely that this job will be a bit too much for the old man of the party. You both have the advantage of ten years, on the right side for you, over me, I reckon."

A deep silence ensued, which convinced me that I was on a loser.

"You're a lousy pair," I said and left it at that. There's only one way then. We toss for it. Heads, I make it, Slag. Flip it."

"You're wrong; it's tails. I'm out." said Slag.

"O.K. Wicky. What do you say? Heads or tails? Heads! Here goes. Tails it is. I might have known my luck."

So I set forth on my back-aching trudge up the hills with the replacement set, with a gut anger at losing the toss.

In a niggly mood I humped the load on to my back and ventured forth on the rockstrewn path, at which the mountain goats would have sniffed a protest. As I looked to the north where Monte Salvaro registered 2,500 feet, to the northeast where Monte Sole hovered at about the same heigh t and to the west where

114

Monte Pigna tipped the skyline at 2,400 feet I bemoaned the fact that I had mislaid my doubleheaded penny.

But the nasty thoughts had only a short occupancy as I thought of the good things on my side of the fence. For instance, the weather. It was the middle of October and it was cloudy and dull; the best for an uphill climb. Snow had not yet arrived.

As the zigzag trudge progressed, a soothing syrup was introduced to my fractious thoughts by way of a two-sided conversation inside my belfry.

"I believe there's a song that goes something like this "This is the Army, Mr. Jones" which I interpret as meaning, as I've said before, "don't knock your head against the ramparts of officialdom. In the cause of democracy you'll lose individualty and you'll lose dignity under the "Yours not to reason why" law. Which must be embedded in every clause of Kings Regulations. Best to adapt the policy of the three wise monkeys. Particularly the "say nowt" bit at the end.

The entire muttered conversation only took up the time I had taken to travel about 200 yards on the mountainside track. I wondered what I would enlighten myself with for the rest of the lonesome journey. I knew something would turn up.

I'd simmered down by this time; in spite of the fact that my knees were under stress. I was not looking forward to the return journey. Knees took less kindly to downhill journeys than for uphill ones.

I reached my rendezvous, handed over the set to the O.P. holed up on the lee side of the mountain and preparing for the next attack on Monte Something or other and prepared to descend.

At long last, on 20th February we moved out from Lagaro and the hill village of Monteacuto Vallese and started rolling westward to Castel d'Aiano.

This short move of about 15 miles broke the tenure of our longest ever battle position and seemed to indicate that maybe, perhaps, after all there was some substance in all the vague talk which had been going on in the Troop for a time. The bushwire recorded, quietly, that our next action would be supporting the U.S. 10th Mountain Divison. Their title was apt enough for the Apennines. The objective; to break out from the two intermediate heights they had taken on Monte Belvedere, advance through the valley of the River Samoggio on to the plains and then cross the last major river obstacle, the Po.

Our Castel d'Aiano gun position was in a field which could easily have been part of the country scene at home; a gently rolling grass field, a few yards from a second class road; with not a grapevine in sight.

Having heard from a mate who had done a stint in the Battery Office that a leave party was in detail and that my name was on it I fervently hoped that the balloon would go up while I was enjoying the delights of the Eternal City. My uppermost wish was that zero hour for the artillery barrage for the breakout would be the approximate time the leave party had travelled 100 miles or so to the south; and unrecallable for the occasion.

The R.T.O. at Montecatini, the spa town and railhead, approximately fifty miles south west of Castel was a rear echelon nincompoop. He only gave us a third rate train and a track to run it on. Instead of Pullman and restaurant cars we had to settle for a kip on the corridor floor and unexpired portions. A poor show for people who had liberated the Eternal City but hadn't yet seen the place.

We knew that an American Rest Centre was to be our heaven; if you considered the prospect of Flap Jacks in syrup through rose-coloured spectacles. Fatalistic as ever, we tuned in and prepared to accept all the alleged cookhouse delights of our American allies. The prospect of a stodge on American rations prepared by cooks from Pennsylvania, Texas and Alabama was an endearing prospect.

As the leave truck swung past the G.I. sentry at the gate, I quite believed that I was entering through the portals of a five day earthly paradise; gastronomically speaking. With a respite from the 178th cooks from Glasgi' and Auld Reekie, the purveyors of the monotonous slosh called M & V, tinned cheese and tinned jam.

The Ponte Cavour appeared in our sights at three o'clock the following day. My left hip bone (I was a leftsided sleeper) was in better shape and harsh thoughts about the R.T.O. at Montecatini had softened somewhat in the rosy hue of expectation. The arduous travel was becoming just a memory, pushed through the window by the prospect of the delights to come. I was in anticipatory fettle to enjoy every minute of the hols.

After all I was a cog in Mark Clark's Fifth Army; an important one I thought, so I was only coming home to my (temporary) ain folk.

Rome offered a glitter of shops, fast moving vehicles, lumbering, noisy trams and all the paraphernalia of a great city. The likes of which I had not seen for many moons.

In the eyes of the Roman spivs, lurking at every street corner and alleyway, all British soliders roaming their piazzas and Vias were wealthy beings. Where they got that notion from I cannot imagine. A sneaked look at my paybook credit and they would have thrown a fit, and disappeared, presto.

Paybook credits were reasonably healthy through being in action for a long time but it seemed that only people who worked in the Quartermaster's Stores could afford the fancy prices of the flimsy lingerie gracing the shop windows on the Via Nazionalale.

"*Sigaretta, Caramella,* sister, Johnnie ?"

The old, old cries assailed our ears every time we appeared on the sidewalks. There always seemed to be an extreme shortage of *Sigaretta and caramella* in Italy but a plentiful supply of sisters., I lay back in the reclining chair in the barber's salon. It was easy to find the haircut shop. "*Barbiere*" in Italian was not a million miles away from the English "barber" so our pidgin Italian was not in this instance put under stress and strain.

The padrone stood back to examine phase one of his attack on my short back and sides, a style I had to endure since my arrival at the 39th Signal Training Regt., Nostell Priory, circa August, 1941.

However, as my hair had always been mousy, insipid and with no curl in sight, I suppose "short back and sides" was the only style possible for me; outside the Army or inside the Army.

"Ay, ay, " I thought, "he's preparing an estimate." I mentally assessed the credit column of my Pay Book.

Picking up his scissors, I knew he had reached his estimate. "What the hell does it matter about the price" I thought. "It's not every day you get your hair cut in the Eternal City and without a doubt it will be the only one in your lifetime. " Knowing the 178th's

117

penchant for "Prepare to move" orders at short notice and thankfully, to date, in a northern direction.

While the scissors snipped, snipped and snipped, my economical turn of mind, enhanced by the fact that I was in a Scottish mob, albeit not from Aberdeen, would not let my mind stand easy. After the tenth snip I closed the mental costprocess. I could not let the thought of mundane money make an obscene impingement on my temporary heaven.

His sleek fingers applied the sweet smelling pomades and the ceremony was a process of delight.

"Il barbiere" didn't mind malingering in a good cause (his); the natives were not exactly queuing up on the pavement outside to claim a seat on his swivel chairs.

Exercising a psychic capacity, a gift usually non-existent to me, I conjectured what he might be thinking; "One third more than normal, plus a contingency fee and plus a cigarette or two;" to cement the entente cordiale, or whatever it was between Italians and the British.

Just his bad luck; I was a dedicated nonsmoker and I knew very well where my current free issue of 50 fags would be.

Where they had been in the last 105 weeks; in the battledress pocket of Carlo Harder, my long mate whose knees had embossed CRH on my vertebrae in the long journey, in the confined wireless well, of the 14 cwt. Humber on the way from Alamein via Barce, Sirte, the Mareth line, Sicily and a whole host of other direct line and divergent points on the way.

It was only when I reached the Forum end of the Via Nazionale that, so to speak, the penny dropped.

"Toc", I ejaculated. For a brief moment mundane thoughts of obscene money clouded out the historical thoughts about the Eternal City. 'Toc' that was a bloody lot of lire for a haircut. I've been taken for a ride ... On second thoughts though it's better than sitting on an upended charge case in a gun pit at the mercy of Bristow's blunted secateurs. "Shucks" I said, going all American again, "does it matter that much?"

Having Mark Clark as my boss for a fair while I was getting Yankeeised and the phrases were beginning to roll, sparingly.

Being very partial to good music I fancied a visit to the Opera House. However, I sensed that "Toc" Kerr was not particularly taken up with the idea in the first place but, like the decent Edinburghian he was, agreed to go. Probably with his native Scottish caution he had assessed the pros and cons of an evening programme which was not really his cup of tea.

"O. K., will do."

So on 23rd March we arrived at the Teatro Reale dell Opera, presented our tickets for the Galleria Centro, Row 5 seats 21 and 22, settled into our seats and prepared to accept with pleasureable anticipation an occasion which was unique in its variosity to our normal lives.

The promoters had, rightly in my opinion, sensed the illiteracy in the Italian language of the onenight aristocracy in Allied Forces uniform, so the programme was specially printed in English, to help the liberators.

The programme included Tchaikovski's Symphony Pathetique while, in Part Two, Act Two of Donizetti's opera Don Pasquale was performed with Giulie Cirine as Don Pasquale and Mario Boriello as Malatesta.

Looking around the packed theatre I could guess that many of the customers were thinking, "Well, at least Tchaikovsky and Donizetti takes ones mind off "recce" parties, guard duties, P.O. reliefs, command post digging etc., etc.," I'm quite sure there was a unanimous opinion that extracts from the opera were far preferable to "two on and four off" or a rendezvous at map reference 646919, in the north.

All coming up again in a day or two.

During the interval my mind wandered to Charlie Troop gun position, juxtaposed between the 6th South African Armoured Div. and the 10th U.S. Mountain Div. and I wondered, amidst all the posturing on the stage by Malatesta, what our very own Mephistopheles, Sgt. Major Jock Cardownie, was cooking up for me on my return to the gun position. I'd a pretty shrewd idea that he would be rubbing his hands, emitting a fiendish chuckle and muttering, with a sinister leer, "Yes, I'll get you. Just as soon as you drop off that leave truck."

It was a certain fact that the intrigue in the plot of Don Pasquale, being unfolded on the stage, had very little edge over that being hatched in the Troop Office at Castel d'Aiano, halfway between Florence and Bologna. It was a cert that you would be immediately advised about an appointment with a block of Blanco and a rifle pullthrough or a big bag of spuds yelling its eyes out to be peeled almost before the distinctive taste of the Roman Naafi tea had evaporated from your palate.

But I had my moments.

Sightseeing, the Teatro Argentina (making two Teatros in three days), Wads and char at the Church of Scotland canteen and the Salvation Army Red Shield Club and the 'piece de resistance'. A Rugger match at the stadium seated, by a show of democracy and the luck of the draw three away from General Alexander.

On 25th March we were detailed to be ready to move at ten o'clock the next morning, heralding the end of the Lord Mayor's Show.

The following day, bang on time, the Muck Cart, in the shape of a threetonner appeared, at the Rest Centre. We said our goodbyes to the arches of the Ponte Cavour, enriched by the shimmering early morning sunshine and started our long trek back north; to the Gothic Line, to Castel d'Aiano and to Charlie Troop in particular.

We were in exactly the same field as when I left; facing the same mountains and talking the same break out talk as before.

As I had forecast, "Jock" welcomed me back with open arms and a guard detail.

The snow began to disappear from the mountain tops and Monte Belvedere, Monte Stanco and the other peaks eased from winter severity to an early spring softness.

On 8th April the G.I. sentry from the U.S. 10th Mountain Division who, at two o'clock in the morning, shouted "Halt, who goes there?" - or an American challenge laced with the same intent - assured me, after I had satisfactorily explained that my errand for the next two hours was the same as his - guard duty - that in his opinion things were brewing up. And he didn't mean tea.

At two o'clock in the morning with a pale moon in its birth pangs and playing hide and seek with the fleecy Emilian clouds wafting around the tip of Monte Belvedere, was a fairish time to sort out the campaign. What influenced us in our assessment of the current military situation was that we both knew that we were peering at the last of the mountain ranges of the Apennines and that just beyond, the Po was the last of the great rivers we had to cross. Two heads, one from Denver, Colorado and the other from Derbyshire, were better than one in putting General Mark Clark's jigsaw pieces into the right places.

Which we did in approximately three minutes; very satisfactorily I thought.

As an associate member of the American Fifth Army I thought I should have a say, which he welcomed. As an American he had a natural right to say his piece about his Brass Hat countrymen.

Felicitations from the 10th Mountain Division to the 178 Medium Regt. complete, we parted at the end of our fleeting acquaintanceship and as I walked round the bend in the road towards the Troop area with the sentiments of my G.I. buddy "O.K. fellah. All the best. Mind how you go" in my ears, the cockles of my heart were warmed.

# CHAPTER FIVE

## The Breakout over the River Po. End of the El Alamein - Lake Garda Road.

On 14th April, the weather was fine and following a heavy attack by our fighter bombers and a great artillery barrage the 10th Mountain Div. opened the offensive on our front.

We lifted the Command Post cover on to the top of George Freddy, secured the brew can, and went careering; leaving the grass field leaguer area as it had been, apart from quite a few foxholes, with its virgin subsoil in an elliptical pattern round the edges.

On the downhill exit road, about two miles from Castel d'Aiano we passed a sad reminder of the loss of a good friend from the signallers fraternity of Charlie Troop.

Arthur Wheeler, while on line maintenance, had been hit by shrapnel while sheltering by the side of a deserted house.

Buried by the roadside, his grave was marked with a cross made with two slats from a wooden box; a temporary improvisation which in its spontaneous sincerity on its lonely site gave poignancy to the loss of a good bloke.

The attack went in against Monte Pigna, Monte Mantino and the adjoining peaks, went of Highway 64.

For the first day progress was slow. Nevertheless we thought that we were getting somewhere.

On the 15th the infantry took Monte Pigna and Monte Mantino and the following day there were distinct signs that the Germans were withdrawing. With the capture of Tole, in the centre of the Divisional attack, the way opened out to Montepastore; and we were well on the way to Highway 9, linking Bologna with Modena.

In four days Montepastore was in the bag, and along the twisting mountain roads we had travelled fifteen miles.

The 86th Mountain Regiment kept up the attack and advanced two miles to Sulmonte.

Although the altitude of the countryside seemed to be decreasing particularly to the east there were still plenty of ominous peaks to the north west. From the backend of a 15 cwt. Humber wireless truck flat land was just as recognisable as mountains. After two and a half years we were experts on birdseye views at the wrong end.

From Montepastore the secondary road followed a winding parallel course with the river Lavino until we got to Rivabella, at three o'clock in the morning.

Despite this unearthly hour more common in the Army than in Civvy Street, which allegedly was the time of lowest physical resistance it didn't matter just then. We were felice, multo *felice*. We opined that if we were leaving the mountains behind at fairish speed then Jerry was back pedalling faster than his normal rate.

So we were, as I said, *felice*.

At Rivabella we really could say we had outflanked Bologna; and after a harsh winter of straining to see the towers and spires of this city which the natives at Monteacuto Vallese had assured us could be done on a fine day, that sure was a lovely thought.

Obviously there had been a scarcity of fine days between October 6th 1944 and April 14th 1945.

Rivabella could be said to be a landmark in our affairs; on two scores. It was the first of three locations to be logged on one day; April 21st, 1945. And it was on a plain; and that was excellent news for the kneecaps.

We advanced to Ponte Sammogia on Highway 9, bypassed Modena and travelled northeast to Bomporto. We had advanced thirty five miles in one day.

The Signallers opinion was holding good. So far.

We must have fired at some targets during the next forty eight hours although I can't rightly remember if we did or if we didn't because Aldegata within smelling distance of the river Po became an entry in the regimental war Diary.

On April 24th we reached the south bank of the Po and the sight of the pontoon bridge at San Benedetto (the second important San Benedetto in my diary), was a heartwarming sight but, and there always seemed to be a 'but', the thin drone of German bombers overhead put a cold douche on our spirits as we moved tentatively over the pontoon bridge to the northside.

123

"Charlie", I said, "Move over and pass me my tin hat. I'm playing safe in these last few days. These German bombers must be able to see this stretch of water like a piece of silvery ribbon, on a moonlight night like this. According to the map I saw in the Command Post the Po does wriggle round the bends here."

My voice tapered off into the thin night air and action took over.

Taking out the tinned milk (unopened) and the bully beef (half used) from my steel helmet, storage accommodation at the back of the Humber wireless truck always being at a premium, Charlie passed it over. I knew it was the right one as it rested on my ears. It had been the right size when issued at Fyvie, Aberdeenshire, in the July of 1942 but various vicissitudes since then, in the shape of hot climates and other hazards in the last two years, had taken its toll on my physiognomy; in the way of shrinking ears and dehydrated cheeks.

I took comfort from the fact that my head enlarging would take place when I got back to Civvy Street and recounted, with due pride and overdue modesty, what had happened to me.

If I could get an audience.

From Bagnolo San Vito, on the north side it was all go, go, go. The whole U.S. 10th Mountain Division had the bit between its teeth and went; fast.

The 85th, 86th and 87th Mountain Regiments moved fast but on occasion not as fast as the 178 Medium Regiment as we leapfrogged the astonished infantrymen.

Military text book theory, which enunciated that the infantry was supported from the rear by the Artillery was temporarily ditched as we left them in our backwash.

Bypassing Mantua, on the eastward side, we kept going and the main road to Verona whistled to the rhythm of the wheels of our Matadors and trucks as we Indianfiled at speed across the plains of Lombardy.

So fast did we move that it almost seemed in comparison to convoy speeds what had gone on before that the cypress trees at the side of the avenued road were the mileposts. No hopping out, into position, and digging foxholes every mile or two; pre Lagaro days, that is. When for six months we kept the same barn for quarters, kept the same Command Post, kept shaving in cold water from the same water tap at the outside of the house, where you knew the guns were in the same little valley, where the stream meandered between snowcovered embankments.

From April 21st the exhilarating experience of fast convoying was like the popping of the cork from the champagne bottle, with its expectation of heady good cheer.

Sadly there was no champagne in the Naafi. So we had to savour the experience and not the taste.

So fast did we move that in our innermost, secretive thoughts we dared to hope that, before long, we would be digging in our own gardens at home. Muscling in on the expertise acquired by the digging of thirty eight Command Posts and scores of foxholes. Shifting in the process, sand in Egypt, Libya and Tunisia (and occasionally hard rock in Tunisia) and heavy clay subsoil in Sicily and Italy.

By such optimism we were prepared to put the opinion expressed in the little booklet "First Divisional Artillery, Anzio, 1944 that "No gunner who was at Anzio is likely to turn to gardening as a hobby" in the background.

Obviously, having had no time to record exact statistical data, we had lost count of the Grand Total of shovelfuls shifted but knew that this item on the balance sheet would have to recognise that in Egypt, Libya and Tunisia, more often than not, two shovelfuls out meant one shovelful sliding back into the hole.

Five miles from Calzoni we notched up another near miss. This ushered in a bad spell for us.

At this time Henry Ford (not the motor magnate) was on loan as driver of George Freddy. He was a chirpy, cheerful guy and, assured us that, as far as he knew, he didn't figure on the same family tree as his famous namesake.

As it turned out in the next three days there was a hoodoo on Henry which did no good at all to George Freddy or its crew.

We came across a straight sided Jerry vehicle abandoned by the roadside and as we had been having brake and other problems with our ageing Humber 15 cwt., we thought of a swop. Having chugged manfully up most of the hills from Reggio di Calabria to the Gothic Line it was hardly surprising that our old friend was on her last legs. There are times when even R.E.M.E. have to throw in the towel and this was one of them.

True to form, on occasion of valueing equipment first (circa Monzuno, just down the road, and the Don 5 phone as evidence) and men second, we discussed the cubic capacity available in the new caravan for wireless equipment, food, kit and men.

With the maximum irascibility that Kings Regulations would allow a gunner towards a Captain, I fired my ranging round and pointed out that after two and a half years I was just a little weary of my six foot one inch mate's kneecaps slotting themselves between the third and fourth vertebrae of my backbone. "Furthermore" I said, getting into my stride, "nor have I been exactly enamoured of having to sleep on Dags (wireless batteries, average weight 56 pounds) in the back of the truck, on wicked nights (weatherwise). At the end of the doss, was embossed on my arse; sorry, Sir, backside, an inscription which ran "Fragile do not drop". As you know sir, we've had more than our fair share of wicked nights lately, so the embossings get more regular."

I was just on the point of saying, "furthermore" again for the next item when the alarm bells started ringing between my ears. "Watch it, brother" came the signal, two "furthermores" in a short session indicated discontent and that state of mind in a ranker can only lead to one thing. An item on a piece of paper which had an important number; 252.

1 heeded the brain box signals, and proceeded. "Then, sir, there's the question of the big boulder back brake." When the b's puthered out, tripping out in rhythm, I thought "good show, Roe, your alliteration is real good. "No joke at our age, sitting on the tailboard, legs overboard ready to slide a boulder under the back wheel when the convoy leader signals "stop" on an incline."

Having circumnavigated in our total mileage round the globe at least three times already usually looking at the world from a back end vista I preferred to end my military stint in an aura of glory, transient as that might prove to be, rather than with a medical certificate discharge caused by a combination of bad brakes and an incompetent driver.

Charlie agreed by nodding his head, thus eliminating the possibility of removing his pipe from his mouth.

So the total committee of four, the full complement of the truck; Captain, G.P.O. Ack. two signallers, gave the thumbs up sign to take the new caravan, acquired from the Wermacht. Now in rapid retreat.

After a mechanical inspection we were satisfied that she would be roadworthy, so, switching equipment, kit and rations we stood around and waited for the next order to move.

At 4.25 the following afternoon we rendezvoused at Calzoni and then pushed on to Moglia where we bypassed four Jerry 170 mm. guns, abandoned on the roadside, on the southern approach road to the village. A great sight. We had logged fifty miles of progress in two days.

The sight of excited natives of Di Sogno, running alongside and throwing bunches of flowers into the Jeeps, Matadors Wireless and Monkey trucks and their spontaneous joy at being free of the Germans, now retreating north in a hurry, excited our prosaic souls. We couldn't translate their rapturous dialetto; we simply translated the happy atmosphere of the sights, sounds and the smells.

"Liberator? Me?", I thought taking in the exaltation all around the little piazza.

"Yes, you, Number 1128308 and a few divisions more." The rejoinder came through the backdoor of my mind.

I couldn't speak for the others but this mental eulogy addressed to number 1128308 the only one I was interested in at that moment, pleased me immensely. I'm quite sure that if, just then, I had been due for a battledress blouse the Q bloke's tape measure would have had to cater for an enlarged chest; sticking out in pride.

Justified, I thought.

Words were superfluous just then but silences can be communicative too and I knew that my mates were on my waveband.

Before this euphoria set in one or two uncharitable thoughts had crossed my mind. I doubted the quality of the celebratory vino being thrust on us and I wondered "How long before they want us out?"

"Liberator, Me?" The thought re-echoed through my mind again. "That takes some getting used to."

But the evidence was before my eyes as the exuberant population clambered aboard or ran alongside the slowmoving column of Matadors, wireless trucks and Jeeps. Flowers were thrown and bottles of vino produced. Each truck had its offering of goodwill; readily accepted. Sometimes the signorinas didn't lose their ownership of the flowers as, in a mood of excitement, they exercised the nicest sort of strangleholds. Mercifully the running board was too high for the middleaged mamas.

Grandads and Grandmas, Mamas and young ones all professing, by words and deeds, that this was the day they had been waiting for. "Include me in on that," I thought. "You haven't waited for it with any more impatience than I have. "

The sight of the milling excited people of this part of the Lombardy plain caused a settling in to my bones of a sense of achievement. Once again I was in my own little world, forgetting the polyglot lot in the 8th and 5th Armies sharing the same feeling. Maybe if we cause such joy then our long marches against Hitler and Mussolini have been worthwhile.

Airy-fairy thoughts about Civvy Street followed each other in quick succession. "Priority number one," I thought. "56 days demob leave. The London and North Eastern Railway Company doesn't appear to have missed me since August 4th, 1941, so they'll have a chance to extend their indifference by another 56 days."

Thomas being my Christian name it was inevitable that I had to be shoved into the group category, 'Doubter'. Only because someone, a rare bird, had knowledge of Thomas, from the bible, and passed down the history of two thousand years ago.

Fair enough, but they failed to assess that doubting in the first stages was the birth pangs of an enquiring mind. I always tried to sort out the pros and cons of a matter; and often came out wrong in the end.

Nevertheless, I had a better track record than the demeaning lot who never left the starting gate of discussion.

What's this got to do with Di Sogno?

Quite a bit. My doubting thoughts were thrown out of the window as I found that the quality of the vino was first class and that

128

the populace was really overjoyed on their liberation day.

For the first time in my whole Army career - correction, for career read 'Stint' - a sense of achievement impressed itself on me, on the lowest rung of the military ladder. And that was very pleasing.

As we moved on I knew that Di Sogno would be one of my very special memories.

Forty eight hours later and still on the gallop to Signore Anons vineyard, or olive grove or orchard, Henry somehow managed, on a rutted greasy side track, to skid the truck sideways on to the verge of a small embankment.

The first thing that Charlie and I knew for certain after we had got over the shock, was that we had been exceedingly lucky not to have had our brains splattered around the inside of the truck from the enhanced weight of three 56lb. wireless set batteries (Dags) flying through the air from one side to the other.

The port side of the truck faced the sky and the starboard side rubbed along the track, quickly grinding to a stop.

We pulled ourselves together and thanked the good Lord that he was looking after us; once again.

Up to then we had been getting on very well with the German caravan, feeling the benefit of the increased storage space and the equipment, bedding, Dags and bodies had a more harmonious existence. We had to admit that the last incident had been largely man-made.

At Rivabella, approximately 30 miles south west of Verona and on the way to our next objective at Villafranca, our euphoria was about to be shattered.

Trying to catch up with the fast retreating Germans, tallyhoing back to their homeland, after finding out that they had run out of defensive mountains, we were moving at a fastish convoy speed. There was always joy in our hearts when the speedo showed a number in the higher bracket. With the mountains receding into the distance our backend view of the flat terrain was not very interesting but we had a good field of vision. The pump which generated our hopes and expectations notched up into a higher gear. But we knew, by hard experience, that we got the exultations and the miseries in unequal proportions.

To a fighter pilot speed of decision and speed of action has to be instantaneous.

So when an ominous speck in the sky got bigger and bigger by the second and was obviously heading for us, we seemed to be sitting ducks. A German truck **in** convoy stuck out like a sore thumb.

Just as the pilot was on the point of breathing down our necks he zoomed away. At the very last second he must have noticed that our Jerry truck was in an Allied convoy. My stomach resettled in it's normal place.

We were part of the Darby Task Force under Lieut. Col. Darby of the U.S. 5th Army and we advanced to Villafranca, ten miles southwest of Verona; poised for the next advance to the approaches to the Brenner Pass, via the eastern lakeside road on Lake Garda.

North of Malcesine the road tunnels through the rocks had been blocked by demolitions. To keep the impetus of the advance going Colonel Freeth, our Commanding Officer, requisitioned barges and the jetty at Malcesine hummed with activity as the 5.5s were manoeuvered on to the vessels. After much heaving on the gun trails the Veronica, the San Angelo and the Ardua set sail and headed north; passing a castle perched on a rock to our starboard side.

The journey to Torbole, in the vicinity of Riva at the northernmost tip of Garda, was uneventful and reminiscent of the peacetime sailings of "any more for the Skylark?" So we reckoned Jerry was backpedalling fast.

The Veronica inched her way in and made a perfect landing, followed by the Ardua and the San Angelo. A DUKW waiting by the lake side winched the guns on to dry land. Operation Veronica/ San Angelo/Ardua was highly successful.

An enemy 105mm. gun, sited in the hills to the east of Arco, searched our area as we positioned in the olive grove. For twenty four hours it harrassed us. We kept our heads low and pinpointed the best cover at speed.

Although we knew that the Germans were streaming back to the Brenner Pass and Austria hard experience had taught us that the darkest hour was always before an enemy retreat when he slung them over to keep us on our toes.

We hoped but couldn't bank on it that Torbole on Lake Garda would be our very last angry gun position.

But so it turned out to be.

2nd May dawned and the soft hues of a spring morning matched our mood of expectancy. At noon we tuned in to the B.B.C. news bulletin and the announcer gave us the wonderful news that nearly a million Germans had surrendered, that all enemy resistance had ended and that the war in Italy was over.

As the news sank in to the four signallers in the little bare kitchen of the house at Torbole, within a pebble throw of a tiny weir on a tributary of the Sarca, there was joy and there was sadness.

An inward thankfulness that the end of a very, very long road starting back at El Alamein on 23rd October 1942, had been reached surged through my whole being.

A road that none of us ever wanted to tread again.

On this day of rejoicing the memory of the lads who would not leave desert sand or Italian soil was with us all. Our joy was tempered with many sad thoughts of the missing faces; those who had shared our hopes and matched shovelful with shovelful of sand soil and clay while digging in.

Thoughts of Bill Queree and Fred Hirst who, by the irony of tragic coincidence, were killed in the same twenty four hours of the crisis period of 18th to 19th February 1944 on Anzio were with me on this fateful day.

On 15th May we travelled back down the east side of Lake Garda and leaguered at Cola di Lazise at the southern tip, a few miles from Peschiera, which sat astride the road and rail junctions which linked Brescia with Verona.

We stayed there for about ten days and as the reaction to the termination of campaigning days sank in life was idyllic; compared. God was in his heaven behind a smiling beneficent sun and just then all was right in my little world.

Little did I know about Pesaro and the Adriatic, then.

Leaves of forty eight hours duration were organised to Venice. They were based at Mestre, just outside the city. The sleeping

*Torbole where the news reached us of the end of the war*

accommodation was of a kind we were well accustomed to; the usual bivvy, in the usual field.

The imitation jewellery hawkers in the Piazza San Marco and the other wide boys in the alleyways waited expectantly to take full advantage of the irresponsible lavishness of a freely spending liberating Army.

Inlaws and relatives, all the way up the country from Andria in the deep south, through Naples and Salerno and via Rome to Florence in the north, had alerted their Venetian relatives to be at the ready when the liberators opened their paybooks.

The Venetians were not blind to the possibilities.

Being cooped up in the Gothic Line for six months had boosted pay book credits by handsome amounts. The vendors of the junk and cheap vino put out the "Welcome" mat, and waited.

They did us no harm. What did the filching of a few hundred measly lire matter when the ending of a war was being celebrated.

Nothing at all, nothing at all.

It mattered not just then that the baubles were cheap junk, that the vino had a suspicious taste of dilution or that the "sisters" were a bit old in the tooth.

We enjoyed the sights while we could. In a nostalgic ego none would deny their pride in the manner of earning the opportunity to view one more historic city. Especially one like Venice.

So I drifted back in a happy frame of mind; well, comparatively.

On 31 May we moved south east on Highway 9 to Pesaro on the Adriatic, south of Rimini.

Pesaro was a seaside resort but in my frame of mind I was not in appreciative mood about that just then. I was too preoccupied with thoughts of demob. I couldn't understand why I could not have been on the first train home after the news of V.E. day on 2nd May.

Disgruntlement was just below the surface but I had acquired a good standard of mental ventriloquism, so "Jock" had no idea of my swirling thoughts.

Pesaro was the birthplace of the famous composer Rossini and this nugget of information encouraged the musical eggheads to try and enlarge their already held knowledge, with the enrichment of the practicality of searching for his birthplace.

The aura of the project alleviated the monotony of the daily round and the common task; soon to be accentuated.

The impact of the Commanding Officer's address to the regiment, lined up on the seafront in the hot sunshine, stayed with us for some time. He had news for us; depressing news for the prewar weekend soldiers and the conscripts. It didn't matter so much for the regulars; assuming they had an unexpired portion of their terms of contract.

It went something like this. I couldn't remember it word for word but I got the gist of it; distinctly.

"Don't think that because the war is over you'll be going home quickly. You are still in the Army (as if we hadn't noticed) and there's a lot of work to be done out here. You are soldiers (as if we hadn't noticed!) and likely to be for some time yet ...

"All right, Sergeant Major."

Mutinous thoughts rippled invisibly through the assembled parade, from left to right and vice versa, from front rank to rear rank, and back again.

"You're all right, Jack." Before I could stop muttering the cliche I realised our Colonel's name wasn't Jack but that didn't detract from the invisible forcefulness of my feelings. "You are a Regular, so you've got to soldier on. But what about us, we don't crave for a lifetime of Army stations. It's time we'd stopped scanning Battery Orders to see if it's our turn for guard duty or whether it's safe to buy ice cream from the Ities. Let's *andiamo* and *presto*.

"Parade, parade, Shun. Deesmiss," bellowed the Sergeant Major.

As the harshly uttered dismissal displaced the close atmosphere of the Italian forenoon and the impact of the miserable news seeped in, the echoing response from the assembled parade was the old familiar cry; "Yours not to reason why, etc. etc."

If, just then, the charge of silent insubordination could have been proved, around six hundred pieces of paper, Army Form 252 "Charges sheet, Soldiers for the use of, against" would have been required.

To rub it in, it wasn't long before we were backpedalling to Cesenatico halfway between Rimini and Ravenna on the northern coast road, destined for guard duties at a POW Camp.

The only bit of light relief occurred when a cheery Cockney Gun Sergeant read out the camp byelaws, for observance by the guard details and translated item six as follows:

"You will patrol the perrymeter of the fence constantly".

As his face bore a resemblance to Stan Laurel it made for a modicum of lightness in our disenchanted lives.

A happy threestriper was our Guard Commander; if I knew one.

To have odd thoughts in odd places was the norm on active service and one struck me, at Pesaro, which might have been feasible.

Our billet, situated at the corner of Corso something or other, had probably been a pensione in happier times. It had a very small garden at the back which was overloaded with vegetation; where an orange tree nudged a fig tree which jostled a lemon tree. There, was difficulty for the light of day to intrude but no doubt all produced their harvest in season.

Could this have been the place where Rossini composed "The Barber of Seville" and "William Tell," I wondered.

Nice thought but there was no plaque on the wall.

A consolation was that nice thoughts, after the Commanding Officer's pep talk, were desirable just then.

Battery Orders were, nine hundred and ninety nine times out of a thousand, a catalogue of military orders breathing fire, details of Guard Duties, postings, promotions, lists of hygienic standards and warnings to any potential wrecker of any clause of the Kings Regulations.

Nailed to the notice board at Cesenatico, about the middle of June, was one glorious exception; a commendation from Major General George Hays, U.S. Army.

The following commendation from H.Q. 10 (U.S.) Mountain Division dated llth June is brought to the notice of all ranks:

1. I wish to commend you and the members of your command for outstanding performance of duty while attached to this division. The work of your organisation was superior in

every respect and materially contributed to the success of the 10th Mountain Davison during the recently completed campaign. It is believed that the close cooperation between the 178th Regiment and elements of this division resulted not only in prompt and accurate artillery support but also in forming a bond of mutual admiration and respect between units of the two Allied countries.

2. A chronological resumé of the 178th Regiment's actions follows:

During the first week in April, liaison was established with l0th Mountain Division Artillery H.Q. and the mission of reinforcing our fire was started immediately. From the very outset the Regiment's brilliant work was noted by our air O. P. observers by stint of the extraordinary accuracy of initial rounds in fire missions.

The 178th Regiment participated in the preparation fire for the offensive at 09.45 14 April. The Regiment was established at this time in the vicinity of Headquarters, 10 Mountain Division Artillery in order to facilitate movements, coordinate fires and procure targets.

After the breakthrough into the Po the Regiment moved always in close support of our leading elements, sometimes ahead of the infantry and behind the tanks in the march column. This support continued during times when no other artillery was available. On one occasion, after being informed of suitable targets, they moved to the side of the road, went into position and delivered fire.

The Regiment maintained forward observers with our infantry and delivered constant close support fire for the crossing of the Po river. After crossing the Po river, the 178th became part of the assault group organised as Task Force Darby. This group advanced to Villafranca in the vicinity of Verona.

In continuous close support of our infantry the Regiment sped on to a position south of Malcesine on the shores of Lake Garda. Upon establishing their O.P., they observed long enemy columns moving northwards on roads on the west shore of the lake. Using CP as an OP, fire was delivered on the lake road. Many target hits were observed and use of the road was denied to the enemy.

When the enemy destroyed tunnels along the eastern lake shore, the Regiment finding itself unable to transport its guns on "ducks", obtained barges for the task. While infantry amphibious operations were under way, no ducks could be spared to haul barges. Evidencing initiative and resourcefulness, the Regimental Commander requisitioned sail boats and hauled his gun-laden barges to the town of Torbole and delivered fire missions protecting our infantry occupying the same town.

3. All members of this command hold the highest admiration for this splendid artillery organisation.

(Signed)    George P. Hays.
Major General, U.S. Army.

In the middle of October the regiment arrived at its last location before its disbandment; the San Remo area in the north west corner.

Regimental H. Q. was based in the Albergo Paradiso, (what an appropriate name for a last watering-hole!) while 309 Battery was billeted at Bordighera, ten miles to the west, while 310 Battery was stationed at Imperia, about the same distance to the east; both places being on the main coast road linking Ventimiglia with Genoa.

Life, for me, at the Albergo Paradiso, lived up to its second name and enchanted me. On two scores; firstly a transfer to R. H. Q. office, with no guard duties, and secondly the possibility of demob in the near future.

As events turned out I presumed too much on the imminence of demob as another six months went by before I humped my kit-bag on my shoulder for the penultimate stage; a Release Transit Camp.

So the wheel had indeed turned full circle. I had joined the Army from the pen-pushers brigade and I would be leaving the Army from the pen-pushers brigade. But, oh, the bit in between. Once again, I one-fingered a slow, and occasionally wayward route on the keyboard of the office typewriter while setting up the

137

skeleton for Regimental Orders and typing some internal correspondence.

Considering that my middle fingers had not seen a typewriter for more than four years and bearing in mind that rehabilitation from a shovel to a typewriter keyboard required a transitional period, I didn't do too badly.

The credit items were on material things such as, no guard duties. Such as, for instance, when seated at the typewriter, by peering carefully and capturing the gap between the trees in the garden in front of the office you could catch a glimpse of the promenade; and say to yourself "I'm at the seaside." And you could have added "And it's not costing me a penny."

By no stretch of imagination did the end of the war mean the end of paperwork but the preparation of Nominal Rolls of personnel due for demob. was a sweetener and it gave me hope. In a relaxed manner Regimental Headquarter's office at the Albergo Paradiso soldiered on. On the typewriter my slow one-finger each hand start had been overtaken by a faster two-finger each hand technique and one result of this efficiency was an increased output and, consequentially, an increased leisure time. Which personal benefit I had to camouflage; not a hard job as the tension had eased since V.E. day on May 2nd.

No longer did the Sergeant Major's beery breath singe my neckhole when shouting "Haircut," (mine, not his!). He too had been caught up by the euphoric anticipation of having a pint on Princes Street in his home town. Sorry, city.

And, on the eve of demob., thinking what a bunch of good soldiers he had on his hands, transformed from a bunch of greenhorns.

I personally, had made a silent outcry about the fact that on my first acquaintanceship with battledress and gaiters the Army was not on my list of likeable employers. I had an initial comprehensive prejudice against all Officers, all Sergeant Majors and a sizeable contingent of Sergeants.

I was as blind as that. I did wonder what the Army could get, to their advantage, from a penpusher of my semi-advanced stage. I'm sure that, in the first stages of my new life, one or two of my

Instructors had been driven near the borderline and only their natural resilience had saved them.

Much, much later on the versatility streak of one certain Sergeant Major, well versed in dealing with greenhouse plants of my type did turn me out to be a fairish example of the end-product that the Army wanted at the exit end of their assembly belt.

In the mellowing experience of action my initial sourings had entirely disappeared. I put the turning point as from 9.40 p.m. on the moonlit barrage night at El Alamein on October 23rd, 1942, when from that night we all mucked in together.

You did a good job, Jock.

About this time the semiofficial Regimental History appeared in the Out-Tray. My first reaction, after reading it, was to mutter, "some historian". Under the heading Alamein - Anzio - Lake Garda this hindsight history had obviously been written by a rear echelon wallah; one of the seven at the back of the real action who looked after the one upfront. Some of the choice phrases could never have dripped off the pen of an upfronter.

Such as:: "A long and INTERESTING march saw us up to the Mareth Line."

"We took part in the COLOURFUL token barrage of Messina. "

"A STICKY PATCH was met at Rionero but a good rest THOUGH IN ACTION, at San Pietro. "

In reality, "sticky patch" meant men and guns bogged down in ankle deep slimy clinging mud. It meant being in a river valley, overlooked by Jerry and at the mercy of their 88s. A real quagmire.

"Here we met 56 and 5 Divs. again one of our BEST BATTLES in support of 201 Guards Brigade."

Sugar on the pill; "We were the last artillery to fire in the 5th Army.

I wondered what General Mark Clark and his cohort of Divisional Commanders thought about this. The cheek of a British Artillery regiment claiming the last-round-up-the-spout-in-anger in their Army!

After a short walk down the Corso Imperatrice, Tino's bar opposite the railway station beckoned; or a short distance further

# CASINO MUNICIPALE - SANREMO

## NEL SALONE DELLE FESTE

Lunedì 31 Dicembre 1945 - Ore 16,30

# Grande Concerto Sinfonico di Apertura

eseguito dall'Orchestra " Filarmonica di Genova "
diretto da

## Willy Ferrero

### P R O G R A M M A

#### Parte Prima

**Vivaldi** — *Concerto in re minore* - Op. III n. 11 (rev. Siloti)
maestoso - adagio - moderato
- largo
- allegro

**Beethoven** — *IV Sinfonia*

#### Parte Seconda

**Moussorgsky** - *Kovanstchina* - Preludio I atto

**Mendelssohn** - *Scherzo* dal « Sogno di una notte di mezza estate »

**Sibelius** — *Valse triste*

**Ravel** — *Bolero*

---

*The freedom of San Remo, New Years Eve, 1945.*

140

on was the Naafi. As a variation, the alleyways where so many of the occupants had an urge to cultivate a contact with a British soldier - for the age-old law of supply and demand could be explored. And to vary the agenda, mysterious but fairly regular trips took place over the frontier into France via Ventimiglia.

These were some of the credits in the boredom of a life waiting for your Release Group to come round. But the overwhelming debit remained. I wanted home to my wife and two daughters; who were growing up so fast without me.

However, out of the monotony of the slow passing days cameth some good. The typing rust fell from my fingers so that, as the days went by, the first finger of my left hand followed the first finger of my right hand on to the keyboard at an increased tempo. Giving the impression that, at some time or other, I had taken a course at Pitman's College.

My transfer to R.H.Q. office was achieved by some influence, aided and abetted by the fact that the regular office clerks, being Territorials before the war started, and recording maximum war service, had a lower Release Group number and therefore were entraining at Milan Central Station for the homeward journey, via Domodossola, Vallorbe and Calais. Plus the fact that the paperwork on which the Army ticked over had still to be churned out until the last day of operations.

The proof of the pudding always being in the eating, suffice to say I was not posted back to 310 Battery.

San Remo had a lot to offer and we took full advantage. We had red carpet treatment from the City Fathers and the regiment, as Garrison troops, got the equivalent Italian honour of Freedom of the Borough.

On New Year's Eve, it was decided that a Symphony Concert in the Casino Municipale was an appropriate gesture for the citizens to honour the liberators. Not the liberators of San Remo itself, as they had escaped German harrassment but the liberators, in a general sense, of all Italy.

If the organisers of the concert had taken a poll of the aesthetic tastes of the members of the 178th Medium Regiment they would have found that lovers of classical music were definitely in the minority; with a preponderance of favour for next door the Casino.

So at the unusual time for an occasion like this of 16.30 hours only the classical music diehards sat on the front seats of honour when Willy Ferrero, the conductor of the Filarmonica di Genova, raised his baton to guide the orchestra through the first item on the programme, the Concerto in Re Minore by his compatriot Vivaldi.

The prospect of *"Maestoso"*, *"adagio"*, *"moderato"*, *"largo"* and *"allegro"* in quick succession had frightened off the rest. Not even the opportunity of a celebration drink on the town could persuade them to occupy a seat on a classical occasion.

Unit football matches and seabathing were merely palliatives to take the edge off the predemob days; but they helped to ease the burden of the wearisome wait for the great day to arrive.

There was a great restlessness to be away, for good.

A nightly trapse to Tino's bar on the Corso Nino Bixio, behind the Ventimiglia Genoa railway line, helped to preserve my sanity on the long wait.

Tino the proprietor, had a billiard table in the bar parlour of his licensed coffee bar.

We were thankful for the existence of Tino and his billiard table.

I had never played billiards before so a whole new world of strange expressions opened out as the advice from my mates on the sidelines to "cannon off the cush", "pot the red", and "go in-off" tripped from their tongues. Their previous experience in a sport alleged to "misspend one's youth" was obviously much greater than mine.

In the process of reaching, to locate the red ball, with one foot dangling, one foot on the floor to keep within the rules of the game, and toes pointing downward, the tearing of the green baize was an imminent possibility as I groped with the tool for the job.

Repeated agonised entreaties, from the socalled experts, ranged from "Take it easy, you'll tear the cloth, that way" or "that was not the way I showed you last night or the night before." climaxed by the caustic comment "Don't some mothers have 'em?"

I muttered to myself, "I'll show'em".

The pendulum was very finely poised for a week or so, during which my jabbing shots sometimes gave me the windup. Tino would have torn his chunky black hair from its roots if he had seen my antics during the first session.

I was saved by the fact that, by a masterpiece of architectural planning (for me), the billiard room was set back from the bar, while a high side partition conspired to play down the sounds of my first endeavours with a cue.

Tino, busily engaged in serving drinks to his compatriots and fully occupied in putting his Italian world to rights, mainly with his expressive hands, did not notice the danger to his sporting property. For which I was thankful as my paybook credit at that moment of time could not have borne the burden of a replacement of the green baize.

Covered by a tobacco fug of which the English proprietory brands contributed at least ninety per cent I lunged on.

Patience was rewarded, however. My night of glory came in the week before Christmas when I compiled a break of twenty three.

Some of the successful shots could have been, without doubt, classified as one hundred per cent flukes. Dame Fortune laughed her socks off at my colossal good luck. For myself I thought I was beginning to show promise.

I had daily walks round the town with Bob. Usually it was on an elongated leg along the Corso Imperatrice, on the seafront promenade, turn left on to the Via Fiume left again on to the Corso Garibaldi and continuing on the final lap at the Via Malteoti, a total trip of about one and a half miles.

So typical of the whole country was this; just set foot on a Via or a Corso, glance at the street name and then step backwards into the past. Via Matteoti, Corso Garibaldi. What history was conjured up by the names Garibaldi, Matteoti, Nino Bixio.

In December the regimental strength began to decline as the impetus in the departure of the Release Groups increased, as the older men with long service in the lower groups got away. The middle aged men with not quite so much service and the young men with service throughout the war began to work up some excitement.

As my own number was 271 knew that my name and number would not appear in print yet as it looked as if eighty per cent of the British Army was in Release Group 27.

When Bob Hutton, in Group 24 left for demob in the week before Christmas I lost a good friend. The remembrance of past shared episodes starting at Dunblane and the prospects for the future had been items on the agenda on our dally walks round the town. Now to become a happy memory. We exchanged addresses and pronounced to meet up again.

Came the day when Charlie Harder was called for release and the overcast sky seemed to be symbolic of my feelings, at the separation from a good comrade.

'H' for Harder was alphabetically nearer than 'R' for Roe on the Release Nominal Roll but having said that, I think he sneaked into Group 26 one before mine because he was a year and half longer in the tooth that I was.

The smell of the ozone in the Solent area was in his nostrils when, in front of the Albergo Paradiso, his name was called.

Not many more roll calls for him; happy man indeed was my longlegged friend.

At the Naafi on the Corso Nino Bixio, over a cup of char, as a parting gift of my originality, I suggested to him that when he heard the Marseillaise, the French national anthem, being played he should stand to attention, for his efforts to support the Free French at Takrouna in Tunisia and when the notes of the Star Spangled Banner hit the atmosphere he should stand to attention twice as long because membership of the American Fifth Army from January 1944 on the Garigliano merited it.

He thanked me in the respectful way that I had learned, by long experience to interpret as "Get lost"!

We struck a verbal contract to meet again the four of us, the ex-railway squad at the fall of the year in London and as El Alamein had started it all the nearest Saturday to October 23rd, 1946 would be sentimentally appropriate.

So the entry was made and the Brasserie at Lyons in the Strand became the map reference for chins to wag.

"If John Hayter had his way," I said "we shall be shouting our heads off at a football match."

As each release party went off, in numerical rotation, there was a joy and there was a sadness as the farewell badinage was exchanged.

"See you in London, Bill, So and so day, so and so month. I've got your address. Don't forget to write, now. None of those desert tricks when you get home. So long, pal."

If hardened soliders ever did have emotional lumps in their throats, there were a few then. Seeing their pals disappear down the drive of the Albergo Paradiso, their last leaguer area. On their way to Civvy Street and all that it held for them.

Early in the New Year individual postings to other units, plus the demobilisation releases, caused an acceleration in the manpower wastage in the regiment, and in due course my turn came round.

The great day dawned when I pulled tight the cords of my kitbag, drew unexpired portions of rations, clambered aboard the threetonner and with a wave of the hand seven of us left the doorstep of the Albergo Paradiso on the Via Roccasterone for ever.

We moved on to 311 Transit Camp at Monza, just outside Milan, for onward transmission to the U. K.

The final curtain came down on the regiment on 26th January, 1946 with the publication of the order "The 178th (Lowland) Medium Regiment, Royal Artillery, ex. 78th (Lowland) Regiment, Royal Artillery (T.A.) ceases to exist and the War Diary closes down."

So the El Alamein - Lake Garda angry road came to an end at peaceful San Remo and we signed off, in the Final Chapter, with the expressive Italian word; *Fini.*

On the journey to Monza, vineyards terraced on the rolling hills and interlacing with olive groves spread out before our eyes to form a scenic pattern of unsurpassed beauty. To add colour to the panoramic splendour the peasant cottages stood out clear white in the midmorning sunshine. The occasional sight of tethered oxen padding along dusty farm tracks added character to the canvas.

With the constantly changing nature of the terrain orange and lemon groves interchanged positions with figs and peaches.

We took it all in, as if to store a picture of tranquility into a corner of our minds, so that when Italian memories stirred in our breasts in Civvy Street we would have a happy souvenir of the country we had battled in. We wanted to forget the charred tree trunks and the withered vines.

At Monza, a Release Transit Camp, I messed about with bits of cardboard, drawing pins and names. One name, one piece of cardboard.

When Sapper Jones, lucky fellow, was pushing the Alps behind him in a beeline for Calais in a Medloc train probably sleeping on the passage floor the introduction card naming Private Smith, as his successor, had to be fastened on the personnel notice board.

This served to establish the correct state of the establishment. I kept the Sergeant Major happy, as I pretentiously busied myself in a job that was a pushover. Everybody or mainly everybody was demob-happy, so discipline wilted a bit in the relaxed atmosphere of a mood of anticipation.

As the blank pages in my little diary were getting scarce, my entries had to be cut to the bone. Sometimes with only a placename and a date.

That didn't worry me as I was blessed with a good memory and I knew that a place-name and a date would be enough to bring the occasion back with descriptive force.

Not that these last entries, in the postwar years, would have anything like the depth of those memories invoked by Rionero, Anzio and Monteacato Vallese and a few others but nevertheless were necessary to fill the canvas.

So the entries read like this:

"Entrained Milan Central Station on March 18th followed by a forty hour train journey through Switzerland and France (like Sapper Jones from Monza, I slept rough on the floor of the side corridor).

Reached Dieppe on the 20th, stayed overnight at the Transit Camp and embarked on the Dinard early on the 21st. Arrived

Newhaven at noon and London at three o'clock. Crossed to St. Pancras and caught the train to Chesterfield.

"What joy is like it? to be quit of care
And drop my load, and after weary miles
Come home, and sink upon the bed that so
I used to dream of: One thing is worth
All that long service; Hail Sweet Pilsley,
Welcome thy lord with laughter."

There is one variance from the original, written more than two thousand years ago by a scholar from Sirmione on Lake Garda, but it expressed my feelings on the momentous day, when at long last I was reunited with my dear wife and two young daughters.

As forecast to Charlie Harder months before, my demob suit did not fit. And my trilby hat was quite unbecoming to a guy who in normal times did not wear headgear.

I gave them both away.

No perks from my Thomas Cook Army tour?

Not to worry, I could remember two cheering pieces to chase the doldrums away from Gunner/Signaller Joe Soap.

I thought of my "Soldiers Release Book" Army Form X 801 which recorded high thoughts from high places. Military Conduct: "Good A steady and reliable man who has worked hard and proved himself energetic and trustworthy."

That took my fancy when I read it, until a niggly thought occurred to me.

Was this eulogy one of the many variations of a mass-produced testimony, churned out to cater for an army? If it was, the ingenuity of the Release Officer must have been sorely taxed and left him panting for the literary variety required for everybody's Army Book X 801.

Unworthy thought, perhaps, but as my Christian name was Thomas, in this instance while not actually doubting I did get to wondering about it. On second thoughts perhaps everybody got the same testimonial. Who would know, they didn't see each others Release Book.

Sweet reasonableness prevailed and I liked it, in the end.

But more to my liking was the memory of the sentence in

Winston Churchill's speech, broadcast to us in the Western Desert with the pealing of church bells in the background, for the victory in the desert.

"You will be proud to have marched and fought with the Desert Army."

I liked the sound of that.